Other Paths *for* Shahrazad

دروب أخرى لشهرزاد

a bilingual anthology of
contemporary poetry by Arab women

Other Paths
for Shahrazad
دروب أخرى لشهرزاد

a bilingual anthology of
contemporary poetry by Arab women

a *Her Story Is* project   edited by Jennifer Jean

Tupelo Press
North Adams, Massachusetts

Other Paths for Shahrazad: A Bilingual Anthology of Poetry by Arab Women

Compilation copyright © 2026 Tupelo Press. All rights reserved.

Edited by Jennifer Jean and Abeer Abdulkareem.

Library of Congress Cataloging-in-Publication data available upon request.

ISBN-13: 978-1-961209-58-9

Cover art copyright © Thaira Al Mayahy / ثائره المياحي

Cover and text design by HR Hegnauer

Copyrights for works by anthology contributors are retained by these authors or their previous publishers.

All rights reserved. Other than brief excerpts for reviews and commentaries, no part of this book may be reproduced by any means without permission of the publisher. Please address requests for reprint permission or for course-adoption discounts to:

Tupelo Press
P.O. Box 1767
North Adams, Massachusetts 01247
(413) 664-9611 / Fax: (413) 664-9711
editor@tupelopress.org / www.tupelopress.org

Tupelo Press is an award-winning independent literary press that publishes fine fiction, non- fiction, and poetry in books that are a joy to hold as well as read. Tupelo Press is a registered 501(c)(3) nonprofit organization, and we rely on public support to carry out our mission of publishing extraordinary work that may be outside the realm of the large commercial publishers. Financial donations are welcome and are tax deductible.

MANAGING EDITOR/CO-TRANSLATOR

Abeer Abdulkareem

ASSOCIATE EDITORS/CO-TRANSLATORS

Amir Al-Azraki
Julia Gettle
Mohamed Hassan
Mahmoud Nowara

POETRY CURATORS

Hanaa Ahmad Jabr
Elham Nasser Al-Zabedy
Rasha Fahdil
Jackleen Hanna Salam

ARABIC TEXT EDITOR

Miled Faiza

CONTRIBUTING CO-TRANSLATORS

Dima AlBasha
Yafa al-Shayeb
Francesca Bell
Martha Collins
Dzivinia Orlowsky
Danielle Pieratti
Susan Rich
Cindy Veach

CONTENTS

Foreword . . . ii
Elham Nasser Al-Zabedy (translated by Amir Al-Azraki)

Preface . . . viii
Jennifer Jean (translated by Abeer Abdulkareem)

Other Paths for Shahrazad . . . 2
Azhar Ali Hussein – Iraq (co-tr. by Amir Al-Azraki and Jennifer Jean)

We Do Not Resemble This World . . . 6
Dima Mahmod – Egypt (co-tr. by Mohamed Hassan and Jennifer Jean)

Good Morning . . . 8
Raghda Mostafa – Egypt (co-tr. by Abeer Abdulkareem and Dzvinia Orlowsky)

Roads Not Changed by the Feet of Walkers . . . 10
Zizi Shosha – Egypt (co-tr. by Yafa al-Shayeb and Jennifer Jean)

Walls . . . 14
Rasha Fadhil – Iraq (co-tr. by Amir Al-Azraki and Jennifer Jean)

The Determination of a Knigh . . . 18
Hannan Haddad – Jordan (co-tr. by Julia Gettle and Mahmoud Nowara)

Neighbor, Urine, and Wine . . . 20
Souzan Ali – Syria (co-tr. by Julia Gettle and Mahmoud Nowara)

My Soul Hungers . . . 24
Raghda Mostafa – Egypt (co-tr. by Abeer Abdulkareem and Francesca Bell)

I Stab Silence . . . 28
Jackleen Hanna Salam – Syria (co-tr. by Amir Al-Azraki and Jennifer Jean)

My Body is Mine . . . 30
Amira Salameh – Syria (co-tr. by Yafa al-Shayeb and Jennifer Jean)

Untitled ... 32
    Omaima Abd AlShafy – Egypt (co-tr. by Mohamed Hassan and Jennifer Jean)

A Pearl ... 36
    Nermeen Al Mufti – Iraq (co-tr. by Amir Al-Azraki and Jennifer Jean)

My Follies ... 38
    Elham Nasser Al-Zabedy – Iraq (co-tr. by Amir Al-Azraki and Jennifer Jean)

How to Write of Love, Part 1 ... 42
    Violette Abou Jalad – Iraq (co-tr. by Abeer Abdulkareem and Susan Rich)

Empty Heads ... 44
    Suzanne Chakaroun – Lebanon (co-tr. by Julia Gettle and Mahmoud Nowara)

Cloud ... 48
    Samira Baghdadi – Iraq (co-tr. by Julia Gettle and Mahmoud Nowara)

Four Poems in Eulogy for My Friend! ... 50
    Faleeha Hassan – Iraq (co-tr. by Julia Gettle and Mahmoud Nowara)

Scarce Air ... 58
    Fatima Mansour – Lebanon (co-tr. by Mohamed Hassan and Jennifer Jean)

Salvation ... 60
    Nesrin Ekram Khoury – Syria (co-tr. by Abeer Abdulkareem and Cindy Veach)

Writing with Water ... 62
    Samira Baghdadi – Iraq (co-tr. by Julia Gettle and Mahmoud Nowara)

Words After Enheduanna ... 66
    Jackleen Hanna Salam – Syria (co-tr. by Amir Al-Azraki and Jennifer Jean)

Repeated Features ... 70
    Suzanne Chakaroun – Lebanon (co-tr. by Julia Gettle and Mahmoud Nowara)

Supplication ... 74
    Suzannah Hani al-Hajjar – Syria (co-tr. by Julia Gettle and Mahmoud Nowara)

The Jasmine Harvest ... 78
Salma Abdul Hussein al-Harba – Iraq (co-tr. by Amir Al-Azraki and Jennifer Jean)

Untitled ... 80
Souzan Ali – Syria (co-tr. by Julia Gettle and Mahmoud Nowara)

The Waves and I ... 82
Elham Nasser Al-Zabedy – Iraq (co-tr. by Amir Al-Azraki and Jennifer Jean)

Manifesto of Voice and Scalpel ... 88
Dima Mahmod – Egypt (co-tr. by Mohamed Hassan and Jennifer Jean)

Revolutionary ... 92
Samira Baghdadi – Iraq (co-tr. by Julia Gettle and Mahmoud Nowara)

Owl in the Middle of a Storm ... 94
Souzan Ali – Syria (co-tr. by Julia Gettle and Mahmoud Nowara)

Eve's Cry ... 98
Suzannah Hani al-Hajjar – Syria (co-tr. by Julia Gettle and Mahmoud Nowara)

Love's Coat and Shoes ... 104
Salwa ben Rhouma – Tunisia (co-tr. by Mohamed Hassan and Jennifer Jean)

How to Write of Love, Part 2 ... 108
Violette Abou Jalad – Iraq (co-tr. by Julia Gettle and Mahmoud Nowara)

The Driver of the Killed Car ... 110
Souzan Ali – Syria (co-tr. by Julia Gettle and Mahmoud Nowara)

Correcting Memories ... 112
Suzanne Chakaroun – Lebanon (co-tr. by Julia Gettle and Mahmoud Nowara)

Oh, Grandma Jerusalem ... 114
Ataf Janem – Jordan (co-tr. by Mohamed Hassan and Jennifer Jean)

Auntie with Two Laughing Braids ... 118
Hoda AbdelKader Mahmoud – Egypt (co-tr. by Mohamed Hassan and Jennifer Jean)

How to Write of Love, Part 3 ... 120
    Violette Abou Jalad – Iraq (co-tr. by Julia Gettle and Mahmoud Nowara)

Pomegranate ... 122
    Souzan Ali – Syria (co-tr. by by Julia Gettle and Mahmoud Nowara)

Details of My Passing Days ... 124
    Khawla Jasim Alnahi – Iraq (co-tr. by Abeer Abdulkareem and Cindy Veach)

Nonmilitary Flashes ... 128
    Hoda AbdelKader Mahmoud – Egypt (co-tr. by Mohamed Hassan and Jennifer Jean)

Siege ... 132
    Mariam Soliman – Egypt (co-tr. by Julia Gettle and Mahmoud Nowara)

Mirage ... 134
    Muna Alaasi – Palestine (co-tr. by Dima AlBasha and Jennifer Jean)

Your Shadow which Looks Like Me ... 136
    Hoda AbdelKader Mahmoud – Egypt (co-tr. by Mohamed Hassan and Jennifer Jean)

The Veteran Strugglers ... 138
    Hannan Haddad – Jordan (co-tr. by Julia Gettle and Mahmoud Nowara)

The Loss ... 142
    Nesrin Ekram Khoury – Syria (co-tr. by Abeer Abdulkareem and Martha Collins)

I Did Not Give Birth to It ... 144
    Huda Aldaghfag – Saudi Arabia (co-tr. by Mohamed Hassan and Jennifer Jean)

Let Us—Together ... 148
    Hanaa Ahmed Jabr – Iraq (co-tr. by Dima AlBasha and Jennifer Jean)

Women of Rain and Silk ... 150
    Mejda Dhahri – Tunisia (co-tr. by Mohamed Hassan and Jennifer Jean)

The Cities' Psychosis ... 152
Suzanne Chakaroun – Lebanon (co-tr. by Julia Gettle and Mahmoud Nowara)

Daughters of the Sun ... 154
Mejda Dhahri – Tunisia (co-tr. by Mohamed Hassan and Jennifer Jean)

Untitled ... 158
Violette Abou Jalad – Lebanon (co-tr. by Amir Al-Azraki and Jennifer Jean)

Victory ... 160
Hoda AbdelKader Mahmoud – Egypt (co-tr. by Mohamed Hassan and Jennifer Jean)

Half ... and Other Things ... 162
Huda Almubark – Saudi Arabia (co-tr. by Abeer Abdulkareem and Danielle Pieratti)

Eastern Passion ... 164
Hannan Haddad – Jordan (co-tr. by Julia Gettle and Mahmoud Nowara)

Definitions ... 166
Nadia Al-Katib – Iraq (co-tr. by Amir Al-Azraki and Jennifer Jean)

Covers of Rottenness ... 170
Layla Al Sayed – Bahrain (co-tr. by Mohamed Hassan and Jennifer Jean)

Middle Eastern Metaphors ... 178
Violette Abou Jalad – Lebanon (co-tr. by Amir Al-Azraki and Jennifer Jean)

They Have Their Stories ... 180
Asmaa Hussain – Egypt (co-tr. by Mohamed Hassan and Jennifer Jean)

The Sad Morning ... 182
Salwa ben Rhouma – Tunisia (co-tr. by Mohamed Hassan and Jennifer Jean)

Comb My Hair Well ... 184
Marwa Abo daif – Egypt (co-tr. by Mohamed Hassan and Jennifer Jean)

Hypothetical Motherhood ... 188
Huda Aldaghfag – Saudi Arabia (co-tr. by Mohamed Hassan and Jennifer Jean)

As in War ... 190
  Iman Alsebaiy – Egypt (co-tr. by Mohamed Hassan and Jennifer Jean)

Cesarean Death ... 200
  Suzanne Chakaroun – Lebanon (co-tr. by Julia Gettle and Mahmoud Nowara)

Birth ... 202
  Hoda AbdelKader Mahmoud – Egypt (co-tr. by Mohamed Hassan and Jennifer Jean)

How to Write of Love, Part 4 ... 204
  Violette Abou Jalad – Iraq (co-tr. by Julia Gettle and Mahmoud Nowara)

The Musician and the Sparrow ... 206
  Khawla Jasim Alnahi – Iraq (co-tr. by Abeer Abdulkareem and Dzvinia Orlowsky)

Hamad on His Way to the Massacre ... 208
  Azhar Ali Hussein – Iraq (co-tr. by Amir Al-Azraki and Jennifer Jean)

450 Dead and a Rose ... 212
  Laila Alahdab – Saudi Arabia (co-tr. by Mohamed Hassan and Jennifer Jean)

A Mountain of Fear ... 214
  Sumia al Shaybani – Kuwait (co-tr. by Amir Al-Azraki and Jennifer Jean)

Guinea Pig ... 218
  Muna Alaasi – Palestine (co-tr. by Dima AlBasha and Jennifer Jean)

The Circle of Time ... 220
  Salma Abdul Hussein al-Harba – Iraq (co-tr. by Amir Al-Azraki and Jennifer Jean)

In Souls, There Are Questions with Wings ... 224
  Eman Masrweh – Palestine (co-tr. by Dima AlBasha and Jennifer Jean)

Wine from the Temple of Ishtar ... 226
  Sumia al Shaybani – Kuwait (co-tr. by Amir Al-Azraki and Jennifer Jean)

The Skilled Tailor . . . 230
   Violette Abou Jalad – Lebanon (co-tr. by Amir Al-Azraki and Jennifer Jean)

On the Go . . . 232
   Fatima Bennis – Morocco (co-tr. by Amir Al-Azraki and Jennifer Jean)

A Shadow . . . 236
   Nermeen Al Mufti – Iraq (co-tr. by Amir Al-Azraki and Jennifer Jean)

How to Write of Love, Part 5 . . . 238
   Violette Abou Jalad – Iraq (co-tr. by Julia Gettle and Mahmoud Nowara)

I Sleep in My Inkwell and Wave to the Distant . . . 240
   Zakia el-Marmouke – Morocco (co-tr. by Amir Al-Azraki and Jennifer Jean)

Acknowledgments . . . 245

Editorial Biographies . . . 246

Poet Biographies . . . 252

for Amy Merrill

Foreword
Elham Nasser Al-Zabedy

أيها القارئ قبل كل شيء شكراً لأنك ستقرؤنا ...

ولتكونَ على معرفة بكل التفاصيل، لا بد لي أن أكون أمينة في نقل التجربة بعدما طلبوا مني أن أكتب مقدمة لهذا الكتاب فعذرا منك.
أختكم إلهام

في البدء كانت الكلمة وتلتها أخرى ثم أخرى وربما أتت بعد تلك الكلمة نقطة للتوقف. لكنها أبت أن تقف... وولدت كلمة أخرى وتدافعت أخرى.. ولم تحبس أنفاسها تلك الكلمة التي كانت بصرخة. فانطلقت بكل قواها.
وانفرط عقد الحروف ليتساقط على صفحات كانت بيضاء تجمعت تلك الصفحات حول الكلمات لتحتويها.
وربما كانت تلك الصفحات في البدء مخبأة في الأدراج ولابد أنه أتى اليوم الذي انتفضت عن ذلك السجن فكسرت أسوار الأدراج وانطلقت نحو الأفق.
كلمات أنثوية وهل يحق للأنثى أن تقول تلك الكلمات؟
سؤال طرح بالماضي ويـطرح في كل زمان ومكان..
لكنه لا يعنينا هنا. إنه فقط للطرح ولا يهمني ما هي إجابته.
سأتجاوزه وأعود لتلك الكلمات التي سطرت فوق الصفحات التي كانت بيضاء فتلونت بأقلام إناثها. بين حلم وحب، بين عتاب وقسوة، بين غضب وثورة. وطن وبيت. حرب وأمان. صراخ ورجاء. ظلم وأمل. أنا وأنت. هم وهن. حقي وواجبي / أين أنا منك، وأين أنت مني / بين أمومة وطفولة، بين نشوة العشق ويأسه، بين حرام وحلال، بين أنا موجودة كما النبات والطير والبحر والشجر وكما أنت موجود.
أحاديث. تساؤلات. مشاعر وأحاسيس. شكلت قصائد وقطع نثرية وحكايا قصص روايات وسير ذاتية.
إنها الأنثى الكلمة الأولى وبداية الكون في الخلق البابلي. من هنا كان لنا الدافع في رابطة لوتس الثقافية النسوية وكادرها النسوي لنتحيّز لصوت هذه الأنثى وما تكتبه، إبداعها الأدبي وشعرها وقصائدها النثرية. وإيمان مطلق منا بأنه لا بد أن يصل لكل مكان ولم يشكل هاجس اللغة لنا معضلة بوجود شخص مثل الدكتور عامر الأزرقي فشمرنا عن سواعدنا لنعمل على هذا والبحث عمّن يؤمن بما نعمله فكان لقاؤنا ضمن مجموعة من السيدات إيمي ميلر وجينيفر وآنا وليتا من

Foreword
Elham Nasser Al-Zabedy
(translated by Amir Al-Azraki)

Dear Reader,

First and foremost, thank you for choosing to read our book.

In the beginning was the word, followed by another, and another, each giving rise to its successor in an unyielding progression. A full stop appeared, perhaps seeking to halt their inexorable advance, yet the words, filled with a fervor that defied restraint, surged onward. The knots of letters unraveled, falling onto blank pages which then gathered around these words to embrace them. Perhaps these words were initially hidden in drawers, waiting for the day they would rise up from their confinement, breaking through the drawers' barriers and reaching toward the horizon.

In every era and corner of the world, the question persists: can a woman rightfully voice such poetic words? It's a timeless query, one that echoes through history without demanding an answer. Yet, in the dance of thoughts, I find comfort in its mystery, unburdened by the need for an answer.

I revisit those once blank pages, now colored with the hues of female pens: dreams and love, reproach and cruelty, anger and revolt, home and homeland, war and peace, hope and despair, injustice and resilience, she and him, they and us, rights and duties, her perspective and his, motherhood and childhood, the forbidden and the permissible, and so on.

Dialogues unfold, questions linger, feelings surge, emotions cascade. From these threads emerge poems, prose, stories, narratives, and autobiographies.

She is the first word, woman. The genesis of creation in Babylonian lore. This conviction propelled us in the Lotus Women's Cultural League to amplify her voice and her literary expressions, her poetry and prose. We held steadfast that her words deserved universal reach, transcending language barriers, guided particularly by figures like Dr. Amir Al-Azraki. With sleeves rolled up, we embarked on this mission, seeking allies who shared our vision. Our encounter

أجل الكلمة والريشة والمسرح اجتمعنا.

نساء لم تجمعهم أرض قارة واحدة أو لغة واحدة أو دين واحد أو قومية واحدة أو عرق أو لون واحد. بل جمعتهم الكلمة فكانت التجربة الأولى بترجمة أعمال شعرية عراقية ترافقها لوحات ومقاطع قصص تحولت لمسرحيات مشتركة بعدما اكتشفنا تلك المشتركات والمقاربات التي لا تختلف بل هي واحدة لكنها بأماكن مختلفة وأمام صدق الكلمة وما تمثله من تجربة واحدة وأن الأنثى في كل مكان هي الأنثى ذاب حاجز اختلاف اللغة ولم يعد يمثل عائقاً.

ليولد كيان جميل اسمه قصتها هي (Her Story Is) ذلك البيت الذي جمعنا توسع، كبر، وزاد عدد ساكنيه ومرتاديه وبين ثناياه ولدت العديد من الأعمال.

بهذا البيت كانت تكتب جينيفر وتجيبها هناك وتتلقفها تمارا لترجمها وتشمر كل من ثائرة وأنغام عن سواعدهما لترسما تلك القصائد لوحات تشكيلية. يحفزني اللون فأطلق العنان لريشتي فأرسم لوحة ثم أرسم قصيدة من كلمات.

تتلقف آنا قصيدة تقرؤها ثم تطل برأسها لتقول لنا كيف أن نعمل فيديو لتلك القصيدة؟

وهناك في تلك الزاوية الدكتورة ثورة تتفق مع ليتا على تجاربهما الأدبية والحياتية على حد سواء تتحدثان بفيديو توثقان به تلك الأحاديث المتشابهة.

بينما تجلس إيمي ميلر عند إحدى زوايا البيت وبقرب نافذة تستمع لصوت فيروز من لبنان وهي تقرأ مقطع من مسرحية نوارس المخيمات التي كتبتها إلهام (أنا) وترجمها عامر. فتحولها لمسرحية تسارع سومة من تونس لترجمتها لعامر إلى الفرنسية بإصرار وتحدٍ.

تعرض هنا وهناك نتمنى أن نجتمع حولها يوم العرض جميعا لكنها السياسة وإجراءات الفيزا المقيتة تقف دوما حاجزٍ. لكنها لا يمكن أن تقف حاجزاً أمام استمرارنا بالعمل.

نضحك عند كل فشل بمحاولة اللقاء الحي ونقول لا يهم نحن تجمعنا الكلمة وما وراءها من صدق.

تتكاثر الأعمال وتتشعب وتنطلق بخطوط كثيرة لكنها بالآخر تجتمع عند حقيقة جميلة اسمها قصتها هي. ولأنها قصتها هي أينما كانت وكيفما تكون فلا بد من توثيق ذلك.

نُشرت ترجمات الأشعار للكاتبات العراقيات من تلك التجارب في العديد من المجلات.

وقبل هذا الكتاب الذي بين يديك عزيزي القارئ ولد للنور كتاب إحدى تجارب قصتها هي والذي جمع بين جينفير وهناء. وكل تلك التجارب كان لها الصدى الذي دفع بنا أن نكون أكثر طمعا وشغفا بعملنا.

خصوصا وأن عائلة قصتها هي تكبر ولم يعد ينفع أن تبقى بين مجموعتين فلا بد من أن يكون لباقي العربيات من مداخلة وبعدما أدركنا أنه لا اختلاف بين نساء العالم فكلمة الأنثى هي واحدة تعبر عما يجول بداخل الأنثى.

واليوم أيها القارئ ومن أي مكان في هذه الأرض ما دمت تعرف اللغة الانكليزية ستبحر معنا بين أمواج كلمات نساء عربيات من مدن مختلفة. ستنتقل بين تلك الشواطئ تمسك الأصداف وتقلب في الأحجار فتخدشك إحداها ربما. وتستند إلى أخرى كبيرة ربما. تمد يدك لتأخذ إحداها ربما. وتطمح إلى جمع المحار وتغوص بين حبات رماله.

وتكتشف أن للبحر لونا براقا بكل أوقاته وفي كل الأماكن.

وربما تستفزك موجة غاضبة ويصيبك رذاذ أخرى ونقاء أخرى وهدوءها فيأخذانك لها طوعا، يسحبك الحرف نحو اتساع

with Amy Miller, Jennifer Jean, and Anne Loyer—a gathering of artists, poets, and playwrights—solidified our purpose and brought us together.

Women united not by geography, language, religion, nationality, race, or color, but by the power of words. This was the foundation of our journey, translating Iraqi poetry alongside paintings and story excerpts, evolving into collaborative plays. Through this exploration, we discovered shared experiences and perspectives that transcend differences, unifying us as one despite our diverse origins. In the face of truth spoken through words, representing a collective experience of women worldwide, the barriers of language dissolve into insignificance.

Thus emerged a beautiful entity, christened "Her Story Is," a sanctuary that brought us together and expanded as more joined us. Within its nurturing walls, numerous projects blossomed. In the heart of Her Story Is, Jennifer would weave her words, Hanaa Ahmad Jabr would respond, and Tamara Al-attiya would translate, while Thaira Al Mayahy and Angham adorned these poems with their inspired artworks. Captivated by colors, I would take up my brush, painting pictures that speak through verse. Anne, upon receiving these poems, would ponder aloud, "How can we translate this into a captivating video?" In another corner, Thawra Yousif and Letta Neely would engage in deep discussions, transforming their shared literary and life experiences into a documented video narrative. Meanwhile, Amy Miller would sit near a window, serenaded by Fairuz's melodies from Lebanon, as she read passages from stories like "Camps Seagulls" (written by me and translated by Amir) and transformed it into a play. With determination, Sou Ma from Tunisia would then translate it into French. These creations found stages here and there, and despite the frustrations of visa procedures, we persisted with unwavering determination. We yearned to gather around these productions on performance days, knowing that bureaucratic barriers could not deter our collective commitment to our work.

We chuckle at each missed opportunity to gather in person, reassuring ourselves, "It doesn't matter; we're bound by the power and truth of our words." Our works flourish, branching into diverse paths, yet they all circle back to a profound truth embodied in Her Story Is. Because it's her story, wherever a

الفكر، والأفق البعيد يدعوك للتأمل.

بين قناديل هذا البحر ونجماته ربما ستندفع إلى شاطئه وتأخذك الكلمات إلى أعماقه لتبحث عن المرجان واللؤلؤ في أعماقه.

عندها نحن غير مسؤولين عن غرقك في بحر الشعر العربي النسوي.

لكننا سنكون دوما منارة مضيئة يستدل بها كل من يضيع في البحر، نحمل فانوس الحب ونمد له يد المعرفة.

البصرة / العراق

إلهام ناصر الزبيدي

٢٠٢٤/٧/٧

woman may journey, however she may traverse, it deserves to be chronicled. Translations of poetry by Iraqi women have graced the pages of numerous magazines, each publication a testament to these shared experiences. And even before this book found its way into your hands, dear reader, another tale emerged—one that brought Jennifer and Hanaa together, birthing a narrative that continues to resonate.

The resonance of these experiences fueled our hunger and passion for our work, especially as our community expanded, making it impractical to remain confined within two groups. Thus, Her Story Is embraced women from every corner of the Arab region, inviting them to share their collective narratives that articulate the essence of womanhood.

Today, dear reader, wherever you find yourself on this vast earth, come sail with us through the currents of words penned by Arab women hailing from diverse cities. Navigate these shores, gathering shells, turning over stones that may either prick or allure you. Perhaps you'll reach out to grasp one or strive to collect pearls, diving deep between their grains.

As you journey, you'll discover that the sea shimmers with vivid hues everywhere you roam. Perhaps an impassioned wave will stir you, while another may playfully splash you with its spray. Yet another wave's purity might beckon you willingly, while each letter draws you into expansive realms of thought. And on the distant horizon, an invitation to contemplation awaits.

Amidst the lanterns that illuminate this sea and its celestial stars, you may find yourself drawn to its shores, where words beckon you to delve into its depths, in search of coral and pearls hidden within. At this juncture, we cannot bear responsibility if you become entranced, perhaps overwhelmed, in the sea of Arab women's poetry. Yet, we stand as a beacon—a guiding light for all who wander within these waters. We carry the lantern of love and extend the hand of knowledge, aiding those who navigate this profound journey of discovery.

Basra, Iraq
Elham Nasser Al-Zabedy
7/7/2024

Preface
Jennifer Jean
(translated by Abeer Abudulkareem)

مسارات أخرى إلى شهرزاد

هذه المختارات الأدبية هي سلسلة من حوارات تضم 77 قصيدة شعرية كتبتها 42 شاعرة من 12 بلداً عربياً في الربع الأول من القرن الحادي والعشرين. وهذه الحوارات هي ثمرة مشروع مجموعة "قصتها هي" والذي تقوده فنانات وكاتبات مستقلات من العراق وأمريكا وتدعم هذه المجموعة مشاريع تهدف إلى توسيع آفاق الحدود الثقافية والفنية واللغوية رداً على النزاعات الدولية ومخلفاتها مع التركيز على مركزية التجربة النسوية.

لقد اختار الفريق العراقي في "قصتها هي" هذه القصائد وكل قصيدة هي ترجمة تعاونت فيها واحدةٌ من هذه الفرق الاثني عشر من أعضاء مجموعة "قصتها هي" والشركاء المساعدين من العراق وسوريا والأردن ومصر وأمريكا وكندا. والترجمة كانت دائماً تتم بالتعاون بين مترجمين من أصول عربية ومترجمين من أصول غربية لتعكس بذلك روح وأخلاقيات "قصتها هي" التي تسعى الى إرساء السلام من خلال الأعمال الفنية المشتركة.

وهذه القصائد ليست مرتبة حسب الموضوع كما جرت العادة ولا حسب الشكل - بل كتبت جميعها تقريباً بصيغة "الشعر النثري" (أو كما يطلق عليه الشعراء في الإنجليزية بـ "الشعر الحر"). وهو نمط يفتح أبواب الفن على أصوات عفوية ولهذا فهو ليس عملاً أكادمياً. لقد صدرت لبعض من هؤلاء الشاعرات عدة مجموعات شعرية وبعضهن الآخر لم تصدر لهن أي أعمال شعرية في أي مكان آخر. وهذا كتاب شامل تمهيدي للقراء الذين يتوقون إلى التفاعل مع نساء عربيات من القرن الحادي والعشرين وفهمهن، حيث يمكن أن تصدح فيه أصوات هؤلاء النساء.

ونُظّمت هذه المختارات الأدبية كما لو أن هؤلاء الشاعرات بأطيافهنّ المتنوعة قد اجتمعن في جلسة رائعة للغاية في غرفة واحدة يتشاركنَ أفراحهنّ ونكاتهنّ وذكرياتهنّ وخساراتهنّ وأحزانهنّ وظنونهنّ وتكهناتهنّ وآمالهنّ ومزاحهنّ ومخاوفهنّ وتأملاتهنّ وغموضهنّ والكثير الكثير. وجرى ترتيب هذه المختارات مثل كتاب شعري واحد تسوده المقاربة العفوية. وآمل أن يستمتع القراء باللغة الإنجليزية كلياً بالإصغاء لهذه المحاورة العميقة ويطلقون العنان لأنفسهم لتندمج مع هذا الحوار التبادلي وروعة الترجمة.

Preface
Jennifer Jean

This anthology is a conversation between 78 poems by 40 women poets from 11 Arab nations writing in the first quarter of the 21st century. This conversation is a project of the Her Story Is (HSI) collective, which is led by independent women writers and artists from Iraq and America, and promotes projects aimed at expanding linguistic, artistic, and cultural boundaries in response to global conflict and its aftermath, with a focus on centering the experiences of women.

These poems were curated by the Iraqi contingent of HSI. Every poem was co-translated by one of 12 teams of HSI members and collaborators from Iraq, Syria, Jordan, Egypt, Canada, and America. This co-translation process—always between translators of Arab origin and translators of Western origin—reflects the ethos of HSI, which is building peace through collaborative arts.

This anthology is not arranged by theme, as per usual. Nor is it arranged by form—in any case the poems were almost entirely written as "prose poetry" (akin to what writers of poetry in English call "free verse"). It is a form that opens the art to unstudied voices. As such, this is not an academic volume. Some of the women have published several collections of poetry and some have never published a poem anywhere. This is a broad, introductory volume for readers who are eager to engage with and understand 21st-century Arab women. It is a house where these women can be heard.

This anthology is arranged as if these various kinds of poets were gathered in a lovely room sharing their joys, jokes, memories, losses, laments, suspicions, predictions, hopes, humor, horror, musings, mysteries, and more. It is arranged quite like a single volume of poetry where intuitive juxtaposition reigns. My hope is that readers of English will thoroughly enjoy listening in on this profound conversation and will let themselves be swept up in the exchange and in the beauty of the translations.

The various co-translation teams developed their own particular approaches to the work with a single guideline to—when possible—let the language be

لقد طوّرت فرق الترجمة التعاونية المتعددة مقارباتها الخاصة لهذا العمل مع توجيه واحد فقط ألا وهو بأن يتركوا الترجمة تكون غير مألوفة كلما كان ذلك ممكناً. فعلى سبيل المثال، قررت جوليا جتلا ومحمود نوارة اللذان تعاونا في ترجمة العديد من النصوص العربية سابقاً المحافظة على فحوى الشكل والسياق ببدء كل سطر بالأحرف الكبيرة بينما قررنا أنا ومحمد حسن إضافة علامات التنقيط التي لم تكن موجودة في النصوص الأصلية لأجل مساعدة القراء باللغة الإنجليزية بصورة أكبر وغالباً ما تخلو المختارات الأدبية التي يترجمها شخص أو فريق عمل ترجمة واحد من هذه التعبيرات المتفردة وقد كان هدف كل فريق في نهاية المطاف الحفاظ على الأحاسيس والغموض والسمات الشخصية للنصوص الأصلية. وأعتقد أنهم قاموا بعمل رائع للغاية!

أيها القارئ العزيز، إن وجدت أشعاراً في هذا المجلد أحببتها فإننا ندعوك إلى مشاركتها. وبالمثل، فإن كنت مترجماً فندعوك الى التفكير في إعادة ترجمتها ونشرها إن أمكن. وعلاوة على صدور هذه النصوص الشعرية في بعض المجلات والدوريات الأمريكية فإنها المرة الأولى التي تصدر فيها باللغة الإنجليزية ولكن ليس من الضرورة أن تكون الأخيرة. وفي الحقيقة إن هذه هي الوسيلة التي يمكن أن تجتاز فيها النصوص المترجمة الحدود الزمانية. ويمارس محبو هذه النصوص الشعرية هذا الفن في سعيهم لإيصال القراء باللغة الإنجليزية إلى مكان هو أقرب ما يكون إلى العمل الأدبي الأصلي. وكما تقول مارثا كولينز في عملها النقدي "في الترجمة" "تعطينا تراجم عديدة إحساساً بالعمل الشعري أفضل بكثير مما قد تفعله ترجمة واحدة حتى وإن لم يتسنَّ لنا قراءة النص الشعري بلغته الأم فسيكون بوسعنا الاقتراب من تلك التجربة".

أتوجه بالشكر الجزيل الى جيفري ليفين الذي آمن بهذا المشروع وقدم كل التسهيلات اللازمة ليرى النور ولا يسعني كذلك سوى تقديم الشكر والامتنان للأعضاء المؤسسين لمجموعة "قصتها هي" آن لوير وإلهام الزبيدي اللتين كانتا بمثابة نبضات القلب الدافقة لهذه الحركة النسائية الفريدة. وكما أتوجه بالشكر الى هناء أحمد التي قدمت الآراء الثمينة وأسهمت في جمع نصوص شعرية لهذا المشروع لا تظهر هنا في هذا العمل ولكنها ستظهر في عمل آخر ربما أكثر أكاديمية. وأتقدم بشكر خاص لعبير عبد الكريم لمساعدتها القيمة في التواصل مع كل شاعرة وحل العقد المتشابكة في هذا المشروع الدقيق الذي استغرق العمل عليه لمدة عام كامل. وأود أن أعبر عن شكري وامتناني الشديد الى إيمي ميريل التي قامت بتنظيم وتأسيس مجموعة "قصتها هي" وقدمت بشكل متواصل النصح وعبارات التشجيع لنا جميعاً ولم تتوقف عن الإيمان بهذا المشروع حتى عندما بدا كل شيء في غاية من الصعوبة والإرباك.

strange. For instance, Julia Gettle and Mahmoud Nowara, who have collaborated on many previous Arabic text translations, decided to retain a sense of formality and occasion by instituting capital letters at the beginning of each line; while Mohamed Hassan and I decided to add in punctuation that did not accompany the original poems, in order to better aid readers of English. This sort of individualized voicing is often absent in anthologies with a single translator or a single co-translation team. Therefore, the many kinds of voicings reflect the fact of many voices. In the end, the goal for each team was to retain as much of the sense, mystery, and personality of the original poems. I believe everyone did a fabulous job!

Reader, if you find poems here that you love—share them. As well, if you're a translator, consider retranslating these poems and seeking publication when possible. Aside from a few American journal publications, this is the first time these poems appear in English—but it needn't be the last. This is how translated poems traverse time. Those who love them try their hand at the art in an attempt to convey the reader of English ever closer to the original work. As Martha Collins says in her critical anthology *In Translation*, "Multiple translations can give us a much better sense of the poem than a single translation can, so that even if we can't read the poem in the original language, we can come closer to that experience."

Many thanks go to Jeffrey Levine, who believed in this project and facilitated its publication. As well, to founding HSI members Anne Loyer and Elham Nasser Al-Zabedy—two beautiful heartbeats of this unique women's movement. And to Hanaa Ahmed Jabr, who provided invaluable insight and gathered poems for the project that do not appear here—but will likely appear in a separate, more academic volume. Special thanks to Abeer Abdulkareem for her invaluable assistance in reaching out to every poet and untangling numerous practical knots in this year's-long, complicated project. And, to founding HSI organizer Amy Merrill, who tirelessly advised and cheered us all on while never giving up hope on the project, even when everything seemed overwhelming.

Lastly, a word about Shahrazad . . . the star and narrator of *1001 Nights*, a series of tales in Arabic traced back past the 9th century. She was the captive

كلمة أخيرة عن شهرزاد ... البطلة الرئيسية والراوية في كتاب "ألف ليلة وليلة" وهو سلسلة من الحكايات باللغة العربية يعود تاريخها إلى ما بعد القرن التاسع الميلادي. شهرزاد التي كانت أسيرة الملك شهريار صرفت انتباهه عن نزواته الفتاكة بحكاياتها الساحرة. وشأنها شأن النساء في هذا الكتاب، شهرزاد تسرد القصص لتفتن السامعين وتبقي على سلامة العقول وتنجو بحياتها. ولكن هناك المزيد والمزيد - فالحياة هي فنها والكلمات هي ألوانها. وفي النهاية، أهدي هذا الكتاب لجميع النساء اللواتي قدمن إبداعاتهنّ الشعرية لهذا المشروع: أشكركنّ لأنكنّ أثَّرتن في فني بصورة لا رجعة فيها وشاركتنّني أعمالكنّ الفنية ولصرختكنّ المدوية في هذا العالم!

جنيفر جين
سالم، ماساتشوستس
أغسطس ٢٠٢٤

of King Shahryar and distracted him from his murderous impulses with her fantastic stories. Much like the women in this volume, she tells stories to mesmerize, to stay sane, to survive. But more—life is her art and words are her colors. This book is ultimately dedicated to all the women it houses: for irrevocably changing my art with your art, and for your bravery in calling out to the world—thank you!

Jennifer Jean
Salem, Massachusetts
June 2025

Other Paths
for Shahrazad

دروب أخرى لشهرزاد

دروب أخرى لشهرزاد
أزهار علي حسين - العراق

مثلك أنا...
منحوت رعبي من دم الصباح
لا وقت لدي الآن..
لافتراش الأحلام
دقات الساعة هنا
ترسم ملامح مدينة عجوز
تنصب مقصلة الأنوثة.
يعرف الصبح كيف يقضمنا يا شهرزاد
زر المذياع يشير لذاكرة أخرى
من فم أغنية مترعة بالضوء
أسافر صوب مدينة من كحل وضحكات
باذخة بحمرة الشفاه
ومثل كل خيبة أنفض رأسي
وأوصده بشال أبله
أحمله على طرقات الكابوس
كتابوت محشوّ بحياة ضيقة
تعالي نلبس الحكاية مسرحا
لدروب الوحل
المدينة تنمو في حنجرتي
فأعجز عن الكلام
يرصني ربها المحنط في لافتات سوداء
ومئذنة شائخة
طفولتي تتكسر على رفات الصحراء
مهرجانات الدم تنبش أعراسها
الوجوه مثخنة بآيات الرعب
وحكايا القبور
لا وقت الآن لأمنيات وردة

Other Paths for Shahrazad
Azhar Ali Hussein – Iraq
   (co-tr. by Amir Al-Azraki and Jennifer Jean)

Like you, my horror is carved by the morning
blood. I have no time to unroll dreams. The clock ticks,
unveiling the old city structures, the guillotine of womanhood.

Oh Shahrazad, the morning knows how to bite us—
the radio brings another memory from a song full of light:

I travel toward a city made of kohl and laughter,
full of red lipstick—like every disappointment.
Stuck in my own skin, I shake my head in my headscarf,
and carry it along a nightmarish road—
like a coffin stuffed with a short life.

Oh Shahrazad, come! Let's put on our story as a play
staged for muddy roads.
The city grows in my throat so I cannot speak. The city

is a stuffed god wrapped in black banners, an old minaret.
My childhood breaks on the remains of this desert,
on carnivals of blood celebrated as weddings,
faces marked with terror, stories of graves.

No time now for rosy hopes, nor to savor the aroma of joy.
No sun tremors with a kiss.

أو ضحكات عطر
لا شمس ترتجف بقبلة
لمن سنقول إذن...
بأنّا للصبح خلقنا؟
والصباح غدا يحمل نعشه
ويفتح مأدبة الوحشةِ
******

لنخرج من اللوحة معا..
لنطل على الأنظار
كل ما تحت تلك الأنظار
يتوهج بدم العذراء المسفوح
الرصيف يلبس قحط العيون
الأفواه تسكب لعنة الفراغ
رجل الغار يمسح وجه هزيمته
بافتضاض الحياء
رجل الغار يرش بذور الرمل
بوجه الندى
رجل الغار يدخن أيامي
في سيجارة عمياء
*****

من يغسل صباح المدينة بالمسك؟
من يوقظ قاتلا للحب..
بعد فرض كامل من الحرب؟
أنحني كعشبة يابسة
أبتلع الدروب بصمتي
أرتدي كآبة المدينة على رأسي
وأطوي جناح الفراشة
تحت ستر الحكايا
فلنصرخ لدروب أخرى يا شهرزاد
الدرب لا يلبس قبو الكلام
وجسد الرقص معا

To whom shall we say, *We were created for the morning?*
Tomorrow the morning carries its coffin
and opens a banquet of isolation.

Let's get out of this portrait, together! Seeing the view from above,

closer inspection reveals the luminous blood of the Virgin Mary,
the desperate eyes in the street—
and from every mouth pours the curse of emptiness.
A depraved caveman wipes his face in defeat.

Callously, this backward man of the cave
throws grains of sand into the face of the dewy
and green. The man of the cave smokes my days away like a cigarette,
blinding me with noxious fumes. *Who washes the morning of the city
with musk? Who wakes up a killer of love,*

after the full imposition of war? I bend like dry grass,
I swallow the roads within my silence.
I carry the depression of the city over my head
and I fold butterfly wings under the cover of stories. Let us cry

for other paths, oh Shahrazad! Those paths are not covered
by the grand vault of sacred speech a man shoves together.
That backwardness cannot coexist with the womanly body that can dance.

لا نشبه هذا العالم
ديمة محمود - مصر

لا نشبه هذا العالم
المصفّحة التي تتربّص بنا تغسلنا قبل أن نتعرّى
هذا الرُّكون لا يعني كثيراً ونحن نفقاً عين العالم بإبرة
العالمُ الذي يقفز كمهرّج فرحان
هو نفسُه الذي يصوّب رؤوسه النّوويّة والنابالم في مقتل
بينما تحجل الانتهازيّة في أمعائه بلا ريبةٍ أو تردّ.
ماذا سيحدث يعني لو استبدلنا نصفينا في محاولةٍ للتّصدّي
وقلنا إنّ الزّبدة نصف المجتمع
وبفرشاةٍ لدهن الجدران لوّنّا نصفينا العلويّين بالأخضر كدعمٍ لمناصري البيئة
واستبدلتُ ساقيَ بعمودِ إنارةٍ لأجرّب معاناة المخذولين
بينما تصبح ساقكَ مطرقةً في يدِ صبيّ خرّاط
ماذا سيحدث لو قلنا: "لا شيء خارج النص"
لا شيء داخله كذلك!
البيضةُ لمّا تزل بيضة
والشعراء سماسرةٌ حمقى بين الواقع والفن
هل أعيرك حمّالة ثديَي الآن من باب المساواة
وألتقط صورةً مع غليونك كحنينٍ غير مبررٍ لطقسٍ برجوازيّ؟!
وما بين "تروتسكي" و"لينين" يمكننا أن نعكس اتّجاهات المناجل لأعلى ونلطّخَها بالأزرق
في اشتغالٍ سرياليٍّ لسحب السّماء لأسفل
واستكشاف ميتافيزيقيا العشرين عاماً القادمة
ونَظّم استراتيجيّاتٍ لمواجهة الحروب والإضرابات العمّالية وإنفلونزا الدّببة
وتنظيم كرنفالاتٍ للإغاثة والانتخابات وجذب مستثمري هضبة التّبت.
عندما رنّ هاتفك النّقال وأنت تذبح فَرخَي الحمام الأبيضين
لم أكن أقصد منع كفّيكَ من الخِضاب
كنت فقط سأقول:
إنّها ليست النّقائض وحدَها ما تقضُّ مضجع العالم
أنا وأنت أيضاً...
بالرغم من أنّنا متشابهين كــنَصْليْ مِقصٍّ

We Do Not Resemble This World
Dima Mahmod – Egypt
   (co-tr. by Mohamed Hassan and Jennifer Jean)

We do not resemble this world—
the armored vehicle that lurks, washes us before we undress,
this complacency means little as we pierce the world's eye with a needle,
the world that jumps like a joyful clown
aiming its nuclear heads and napalm fatally
while corruption gallivants in its guts without doubt or hesitation.
What would happen if we swapped our halves, attempting confrontation,
and said that butter is half of society,
and with a mural brush painted our upper halves green to support environmentalists,
and I replaced my legs with lamp posts to know the plight of the betrayed,
while your legs become a hammer in the hand of an apprentice?
What would happen if we said: *Nothing outside the script!*
Nothing inside it either!
The egg is still an egg,
and poets are foolish brokers between reality and art.
Should I lend you my bra now in the name of equality,
take a photo with your pipe as unjustified nostalgia for a bourgeois ritual?
Between "Trotsky" and "Lenin" we could reverse the sickles upwards, splash them with blue
in a surreal effort to pull the sky down,
to explore the metaphysics of the next twenty years,
and strategies to face wars, labor strikes, and bear flu.
Organize carnivals for relief, elections, and attracting investors from Tibet.
When your cell phone rang as you slaughtered two white pigeons,
I did not mean to prevent your hands from being stained with blood.
I was just going to say:
It is not only contradictions that disturb the world's order,
It's you and me too . . .
Despite us being as similar as the blades of scissors!

صباح الخير
رغدة مصطفى - مصر

لعناقيد العنب المتدلية من أسطح البنايات
صباح الخير
لثياب الفلاحات المزركشة يتجولن بها في زحام الأسواق وضجيجها
صباح الخير
للأغنيات المتسربة من الميكروباصات وسط السباب والفوضى
صباح الخير
للزهور الصغيرة النابتة على جانبي الطرق السريعة
صباح الخير
للعيون الكحيلة الناعسة لصائد اليمام
صباح الخير
للجمال الطليق لا يتمنع ولا يملكه أحد

Good Morning
Raghda Mostafa – Egypt
(co-tr. by Abeer Abdulkareem and Dzvinia Orlowsky)

Good morning

To the grape clusters overhanging from rooftops

Good morning

To adorned clothes of peasant women wandering in noisy, crowded markets

Good morning

To songs seeping from microbuses surrounded by curses and chaos

Good morning

To small flowers sprouting on highway sidewalks

Good morning

To the black, sleepy eyes of a dove's hunter

Good morning

To unfettered beauty that can't be denied or owned

طرق لم تغيرها أقدام السائرين
زيزي شوشة - مصر

ليس لي ماضٍ
ولا أستطيع أن أضع قدمي،
في أيام مظلمة
لا قاع لها
سأحتسي الليل البارد،
وأطفئ النهار بحفنة من التراب،
ثم أقف ثابتة
لأحدثكم عني،
أعرف
هواء ثابتا،
طرقا لم تغيرها أقدام السائرين،
حزنا يخرج من حقيبتي
وملابسي التي ترفض السقوط،
رغم أنها لا تعرفني بما يكفي
أعرف رجلا أصيب بالعمى،
من كثرة تحديقه في العالم،
وامرأة يزورها الموت كل ليلة،
ولا يتركها دون أن ينتزع
خصلة من شعرها،
وحين تصحو
تخرجُ الحياة من ثوبها
كرغيف ساخن،
أعرف جيدا
الصمت الذي يغلق الأبواب،
والجوع الذي يزحف في الطرقات،
بحثا عن الأحياء الفقيرة،

Roads Not Changed by the Feet of Walkers
Zizi Shosha – Egypt
   (co-tr. by Yafa al-Shayeb and Jennifer Jean)

I have no past roads. And I can't put my feet up
on dark days
with endless freefalls.
I drink a cold night

and quench my noons with a handful of dirt.
Then I stand still
to chat with you about me—about
petrified air,

roads not changed by the feet of walkers,
sadness escaping the body of my purse,
these familiar clothes
that refuse to leave me

though they do not know me. I know
a man who was blinded
by staring at the world too much, and a woman
who is visited by death every night. Death

does not leave her without removing a lock
of her hair, and when she wakes—life
springs from her robe
like a hot loaf. I know

أعرف الكثير عن السماء الفارغة،
والأرض التي صارت حفرة،
لكنني لا أعرف شيئا
عن دمي
الذي كتب
هذه القصيدة

very well the silence that shuts a door,

and the hunger that creeps like a scent in the streets

in search of a slum.

I know a lot about empty skylines

and the land that has become

a hollowed belly.

But I do not know anything about my life-

blood that writes this poem.

جدران
رشا فاضل - العراق

جدار ١

هكذا أصبح لجلدي ألوان وأعلام..
وشعارات تشاكس الشمس ببريقها
وقبل ذلك كنت لا أرتدي إلا عرائي
كنت أحك جلد الكلاب السائبة كأحلامي
وأحنو على تكوّر عظامها على الخواء
كانت تلاحق العابرين..
كان العابرون يخافونها.. يخافوننا..
وحدي كنت أمسد عراءها الذي يشبه عرائي
ووحدي كنت أفهم عواءها.
كان الصباح يدق جسدي بأهازيج العابرين
وهم يرقبون الشعارات المعلقة فوق جفوني
شعارات حمراء.. بيضاء وأخرى زرقاء
حتى وجدتني في مهرجان حافل بالألوان..
بريق له رائحة العيد..
وحدها الكلاب التي كانت تؤنس وحدتي
لم تعد تشاطرني الليل والسأم واللعنات..
كانت تمر من أمامي وحيدة مستوحشة..
وحين أردت أن أناديها
اختنق صوتي..
وأضاع الدرب إليهم..
وتذكرت حينها...
أنني جدار

Walls
Rasha Fadhil – Iraq
   (co-tr. by Amir Al-Azraki and Jennifer Jean)

Wall #1

That's how my skin became colors and flags,
with slogans that wrangle with the sunshine.
Before that, I only wore my nakedness.
I scratched the skin of stray dogs, like my dreams.
I bent over their bones, curling up on the emptiness.
They chased passersby.
Passersby were afraid of them, of us.
Alone, I held their nakedness, which looks like mine.
Alone, I understood their howl.
The morning hammered my body with their election songs,
which watch the slogans hanging above my eyelids.
Red logos, white and blue—
I found myself in a colorful festival,
with a glamour that has the smell of Eid.
Even the dogs who used to cuddle my loneliness
no longer shared the night, the boredom, the curses.
They passed in front of me, lonely and lonesome.
And when I wanted to call them,
my voice choked,
lost its way to them.
Then, I remembered . . .
I'm a wall.

جدار ٢

كان دفء جسديهما المتلصقين يثير الأسئلة في جسدي المنذور للانتظار والصمت..
كان يدفعها إلى جسدي دون أن يدري أني أضاجع عطشي بها
كانا يلهثان الحب..
وكنت ألهث عجاف سنواتي الألف..
كنت أتلمس نبضها وهو ينساب بين شقوق عطشه
كانت تتلو صلواتها عند جدوله
كان يلتهم بياضها مسامة تلو أخرى
كانت تهمس له " كم أحبك "
غير أن همسها كان يصطدم بجدار فحيحه " كم اشتهيكِ "
وكنت أريد أن أسور ليلى لأحميها من الذئب
لكن يدي خذلتني أيضا
فقد كنت.. جدارا.

جدار ٣

أنا المنذور منذ عصور للأمنيات المستحيلة
للأدعية التي لم ترتفع شبرا عن قمة أحجاري
لإعادة حبيبها الغائب
لإستدراج طفلها العالق برحم السماء منذ عمر
أنا الماثل بين الرجاء والدمعة..
أحمل ثقل أحلامهم وأمنياتهم التي تتعلق في عنقي كل يوم..
أنا العاجز عن فك قيود أحلامهم التي يعلقونها في رقبتي كل عيد
أنا العاجز عن تنشق الشمس منذ عصور
أقف في مكاني منذ زمن الدمعة الأولى.
ولا أجرؤ على كسرخزف قلوبهم الشاخصة نحوي.
رغم أني.. جدار

Wall #2

The warmth of their bodies touched me,
raised questions in my body, which is pledged to patience, to silence.
He pushed her into my body, not knowing I fulfilled my thirst through her.
They gasped at love.
And I gasped my thousand lean years.
I felt her pulse flow into the cracks of his thirst.
She recited her prayers at his creek.
He devoured her whiteness, one pore at a time.
She whispered to him, *How much I love . . . !*
And this whisper hit the wall of his hiss, *How much I desire . . . !*
I want to fence in Laila, to protect her from this Wolf,
but my hands fail me
because I'm a wall.

Wall #3

I am a vow for ages for impossible wishes.

For prayers that did not rise to the top of my stones
to bring back her absent lover,
to pull out her child who has been stuck in the womb since ages,
I am the one between hope and tears.
I carry the weight of their dreams and wishes,
hung on my neck every day.
Unable to untie the chains of their dreams from my neck every Eid.
Unable to breathe in the sun for ages.
I stand in my place since the time of the first teardrop.
And I dare not shatter their porcelain hearts gazing toward me,
even though I am a wall.

إصرارُ فارس
حنان حداد - الأردن

سَائرٌ بالـدَربِ حائرٌ تائهٌ الخطى والهُـدى دَلـيـل
مُدرِكٌ أنَّ الطَريقَ وَعرٌ غَيرُ مُعبَّد وجِدًّا طَويل
وليسَ بجُعبَتي إلّا القَليلُ وبَعضُ نورِ فَتيل
أمّا العَـزمُ حِملُ جَمّالٍ ثَقـيل جداً جَميل
التَـصميمِ أشَـدهُ لِنيلِ المُبتَغى والهَدف جَليل
وإصـرارُ فَـارسٍ امتَطى بِعُنفـوانِ ذَاكَ الأصيل
وخُطى تتَهادى راسِخةً حالمةً بأمَلٍ يَبدو ثَقيل
لارتِقاءِ سُلمِ الحياةِ صُعوداً وَحيداً دونَ مُعيل
إنَّهُ انتِصارٌ لوصُول القمة بَعيداً عن كلمة مُستَحيل

The Determination of a Knight
Hannan Haddad – Jordan
(co-tr. by Julia Gettle and Mahmoud Nowara)

Walking along the path, confused, lost
And guidance is proof
Realizing that the road is rough, unpaved
And very long
And I have but little up my sleeve
Just a light fuse
As for determination, it is a heavy burden of beauty
Very beautiful
Resolve is the surest way to achieve what is desired
And the goal is great
And the determination of a knight who mounted vigorously
That thoroughbred
And footsteps wander steadily, dreaming of hope
It seems heavy
To climb the ladder of life alone
Without a breadwinner
For it is a victory to reach the peak far from
The word impossible

الجار والبول والخمر
سوزان علي - سوريا

عندي حانة صغيرة
دون اسم أو لافتة
أربع طاولات دون كراسٍ
وزجاجات فارغة للذكريات
ولدي خطوط متعرجة على الجدران
كتبتها الحرب:
"لا تنسني يا وقح"
"من كثر شوقي سبقت عمري"
وعندي روزنامة من المسجد القريب
وسبحة بيضاء من الكنيسة القريبة
وقلم رصاص من شاعر انتحر شنقا منذ مدة
وليمونة صفراء من الله.
حانتي فارغة هذا العام
حيث الوباء طعن الخطوات إلي
لا لا لم يخافوا
زبائني شجعان
لقد ماتوا
ماتوا دون أن يساعدوني في إصلاح الحمام
أحدهم وكان ضابطا متقاعدا
وعدني بأنه سيفتح لي مجرى الصرف الصحي
بطريقة سحرية
لكنه مات أيضا.
كل ليل
أجلس وحيدة في حانتي
أملأ كؤوس الخمر بالماء العكر
وأحدق في ظلال المارة

Neighbor, Urine, and Wine
Suzanne Ali – Syria
   (co-tr. by Julia Gettle and Mahmoud Nowara)

I have a small bar
Without a name or sign
Four tables without chairs
And empty bottles for memories
And I have winding lines on the walls
Written by the war:
"Don't forget me, you jerk."
"So much was my longing, I surpassed my life."
And I have a calendar from the nearby mosque
And a white rosary from the nearby church
And a lead pencil from a poet who committed suicide by hanging a while ago
And a yellow lemon from God.
My bar is empty this year
Since the pandemic stabbed the steps to me
No, no, they were not afraid
My clients are brave
They have died
They died without helping me fix the bathroom
One of them was a retired officer
He promised me that he would open the sewer for me
In magical fashion
But he died too.
Every night
I sit alone in my bar
Fill wine glasses with the murky water
And I stare at the shadows of the passersby

يا إلهي
الحانة لا تحتمل هذه الحياة
وجاري البدين
يهدد الجمهورية ليلا ونهارا
بإغلاق حانتي وروائحها الكريهة
وحنفية الحمام تصفر وتصفر
ربما بدأت الحرب
مرة أخرى
دون ضيوف يقرؤون لي الشعر
ويشتمون الحب
ويذكرون العاهرات بكلام مقدس.

Oh, my God
The bar can't bear this life
And my fat neighbor
Threatens the republic day and night
With closing my bar and its hateful smells
And the bathroom faucet hisses and hisses
Maybe the war has begun
Once again
Without guests reading poetry to me
And boasting of love
And recalling prostitutes with sacred words.

روحي جائعة
رغدة مصطفى - مصر

أشاهد أفلامًا، اقرأ كتبا، وأستمع للأغاني
وتواصل عواءها
ألتهم دفعات من الجمال والمعرفة
وقبل هضمها تمامًا، أجوع
وأطلب المزيد والمزيد
مرات يصل الهوس للحد الذي يدفعني
إلى فتح كتاب على خلفية موسيقية بينما أتابع فيلما.
المحصلة صفر
الشبع لا يأتي ولا سلام.

"كلٌ جعلنا من اسمه نصيبا"*
سنتغاضى عن المجاز ونفسره حرفيًّا
أرغب بنصيبي فيه منك
أنطق اسمي على مهل
لأقطفه من فمك حرفا حرفا.
ربما أشبع ويثمر بداخلي.

لم ينطق أحد اسمي بطريقة أحبها يوما
لأحس بوجودي لحظة نطقه.

توقف فقط توقف لا تردده مرة أخرى
النهم تبدل إلى فتور.

أحتاج إلى المشي وحيدة بلا وجهة
الشعور بالهواء يحرك ثيابي

My Soul Hungers
Raghda Mostafa - Egypt
(co-tr. by Abeer Abdulkareem and Francesca Bell)

I watch movies, read books, and listen to songs
and its howling continues
I devour batches of beauty and knowledge
and before fully digesting them, I'm hungry
and ask for more and more
Sometimes obsession grows so strong it drives me
to open a book, music on in the background, while watching a film
The result is nothing
Neither satiation nor peace arrive

Everyone possesses a portion of their name's meaning
We will ignore the metaphor and explain it literally
I want my portion of it from you
Pronounce my name slowly
to assemble it letter by letter
Perhaps I'll be sated and it will bear fruit inside me
Not once has anyone pronounced my name as I like it
so that my presence is palpable at the moment of articulation

Stop, just stop, don't repeat it
Greed has changed to indifference

I need to walk alone without destination
to feel air stirring my clothes
to look at trees, the colorful flowers and fruit along the road

النظر إلى الشجر، ألوان الزهر والثمار طول الطريق
سماع زقزقات العصافير المحتدة قبل الغروب
أترك للجمال استيطاني
بلا أفكار بلا أي أفكار
حين يرهقني المشي
أستقل عربة استمع لأغاني سائقها
إذا أعجبتني،
سأدعه يُخمن الطريق إلى البيت.

to hear the impassioned chatter of sparrows at sunset
to let beauty dwell in me
without thoughts, without any thoughts at all
When walking wears me down
I'll climb into a carriage and listen to its driver's songs
If I like them
I'll let him figure out the way home

أطعنُ الصمتَ
جاكلين سلام - سوريا

أطعنُ الصمتَ ألف مرة ومرة
أحبيه ولا أقتله كله
بين طياته كتبي المضمرة
وقد تجمّدت بعضها
وأخرى تنزف على الورق

حين انزاحت العتمة تحررت أشواق الأجساد
بيننا قلق اليقين وغابات بلا نهاية
يتعقبنا الموت الذي لا يشيخ
يأخذنا إلينا ويقفل باب السؤال
أمدّ لساني إلى فمكَ
أوقظُه
نتكلّمْ كي لا ترجمنا المجرة بما تبقى من حجر يدور ويطحن المعاني
لا أحد يموت من رغبات الكلمات المخزونة
لشدّة الشغف، يحلّقُ قلبي نحو قباب القلوب، كأنني ما حملتُ في فمي الأنهار وعلى رأسي حقائب الغربة

الأيام كتبنا المُلقاة في الأرض
الكلمات ثمار جنّة العقل ومنها تسيل روح الفرد في قطرات الحبر

I Stab Silence
Jackleen Hanna Salam – Syria
(co-tr. by Amir Al-Azraki and Jennifer Jean)

I stab silence a thousand times and again.
I revive it and do not kill it completely.
Within its folds lie my inner thoughts,
some frozen, while others bleed onto paper.

When darkness recedes, the longings of bodies are set free.
Between us is the anxiety of certainty and endless forests.
Death, which does not age, pursues us.
It leads us to ourselves and closes the door of questioning.
I extend my tongue to your mouth,
I awaken it.

We speak so the galaxy does not stone us with remaining stones
rotating and grinding meanings.
No one dies from the desires of stored words.
My heart soars passionately toward the dome of the heart,
as if I didn't carry rivers in my mouth and the exile's bags on my head.
Days are our books, scattered in the universe.
Words are the fruits of the mind's garden
from which one's soul flows like ink.

جسدي لي
أميرة سلامة - سوريا

في تلك اللّيلة
باغتَ البرقُ مرآتي
فرأيتُني عارية
عن غير قصدي
كأنّي لم أعرفني
بلا أقمشة؟
فرقعَ رعدٌ
انهمرَ مطرٌ
أُرسِلَ من جديد برقٌ
وما أزال واقفة أتأمَّلني
دون أن أخجل منّي
لقد سئمتُ العتمَ
يلتهمُ البرقَ
ومرآتي
ويلتهمني

My Body is Mine
Amira Salameh – Syria
(co-tr. by Yafa al-Shayeb and Jennifer Jean)

In that dark, the light
strike startled my mirror.
I saw nudity—by accident—
and did not understand myself
without fabric.
Thunder boomed and rain released
bright streaks—again, again. And,
I froze. Stared
openly—exhausted
by dark devouring
lightning, my mirror,
me.

بدون عنوان
أميمة الشافي - مصر

١

في المرة الأولى؛
أخرجت الطبيبة طفلا مني
كان ذلك حين قرر الجنين بحسم:
"لن أكون كائنا طفيليا بعد الآن؛ لقد اكتفيت من التنطع"
هكذا،
كانت البيولوجيا تخبرنا دائما بكل شيء
بالبساطة المتوقعة من العلوم.
في المرة الثانية؛
أخرج الطبيب شريكا في الجريمة
كان ذلك حين قرر جسدي أن يكف عن الكذب والاحتمال
عن التضخم والألوهية المصطنعة
بالبساطة المعقدة
لرحم اكتشف حقيقته الفاجرة
فقرر الانتحار تكفيرا عن خطاياه
أو لأنه قد تعب أخيرا من ادعاءات القداسة المزيفة.

٢

أريد أن أكتب عن الحب
أتبع ألعاب الخيال مثلما يفعل الجميع
أستخدم التشبيهات القديمة
وأصف التفاصيل
لكن هذا لا يغويني بما فيه الكفاية

Untitled
Omaima Abd AlShafy – Egypt
(co-tr. by Mohamed Hassan and Jennifer Jean)

1

The first time
the doctor pulled a baby from me,
my baby decided:
"I will not be parasitic, I'm done with loitering!"
And so,
biology told the truth
with the frankness of all Science.
The second time,
the doctor pulled an accomplice from me.
My body'd stopped lying, putting up with pain,
bloating, and claiming fake divinity.
With the complex simplicity
of a womb discovering its wicked truth,
my womb committed suicide to atone for its sins.
Or maybe it was tired of claiming fake sanctity.

2

I want to write about love.
I follow the games of fantasy, like everybody.
I use stock tropes.
I describe the details.
Yet, I'm unsatisfied.

أريد أن أجرب الحب أكثر
حبا قويا، كجرعة من مشروب أو مخدر جيد
تأتي في الوقت المناسب بالضبط
فتملأ تجاويف روحك بفقاعات ملونة
لا تعرف ساعتها من أين يأتي الضوء
ولا من أين تتسرب البهجة
الغواية هي أم الحب
تصنعه على مهل، وترسم مستقبله
لكنها تظل أكثر متعة منه
ربما تنمو الغواية في الخيال فعلا
وربما تصنع الحب فعلا
لا يهم
يكفينا أن نطفو قليلا
قليلا فقط.

٣

سألني الطبيب في تهذيب كبير، لماذا تحتملين الألم؟
فكرت للحظة أن أنكر احتمالي لأي ألم؛
أنا -كما أعرفني- لا أحتمل الألم بأي شكل كان،
لكنني تراجعت عن الرد،
فكرت فقط أن الآلام لصيقة بنا -نحن النساء-
وما نسميه حياة يومية يسمونه احتمالا!

I want more of love.
Passionate love, like wine or pills
coming at just the right moment,
filling the hollows of the soul with colorful bubbles
when you don't know the source of all light.
Or how ecstasy seeps away.
and seduction, the mother of love,
leisurely creates, charts its future.
Remains, absolutely, gratifying.
Yet, it's possible, seduction thrives in fantasy.
And, maybe, it makes actual love . . .
Anyways.
It's enough that we float a little.
Just a little!

3

The doctor asked, politely, "Why do you put up with pain?"
And, for a moment, I considered denial.
Because I know myself, know I don't tolerate any agony.
But I decided to shut up.
I also know pain is a woman's forever friend.
What we call daily living, men call awful endurance!

لؤلؤ
رمين المفتي - العراق

كحبة رمل،
ينغرس الانتظار
في قلب
يحيطها بالدموع.
تفرزها العين
لؤلؤة،
تخطفها يد
مترعة بالعسل،
متعجبة
أن تفرز العين المنتظرة
لؤلؤا..

A Pearl
Nermeen Al Mufti – Iraq
(co-tr. by Amir Al-Azraki and Jennifer Jean)

Like sand,
waiting is ingrained
in her heart, is encircled
by tears—those pearls
dropped from an eye . . .
A pearl—snatched by
an insensitive, honeyed
hand—is rudely
awakened!
How could the waiting eye
continue
to shed pearls?!

حماقاتي
إلهام ناصر الزبيدي

يحدث الآن
أتجاهل الإصغاء لحديث الرياح مع خصلات شعري
أغض النظر
عن حاجتي لجلستنا الصباحية برفقة فنجان القهوة
أصم أذني
عن زعردة العصافير
ومحاولة بائسة لإشغالي عنك
أصوب نظري
نحو سرب حمام
يتنقل بين شرفات المنازل
أتابعه أتابعه
يختفي السرب
وتعود أنت
....
وحده هدوء المكان يقتحمني
يفجر بداخلي ألف لوعة
يحاول الوصول إليك
يمد لسانه السحري
كي يمسح صخب وجودك
ويمحي حيرتي
يغور بالعمق
يغور
يغور
ولأني أتقن إخفاءك
يلملم خيبته وينسحب

My Follies
Elham Nasser Al-Zabedy – Iraq
   (co-tr. by Amir Al-Azraki and Jennifer Jean)

I stop listening to the wind with my hair.
I turn from
my need for our mornings, our cups of coffee.
I stop listening
to the chirps of any birds,
and in a futile attempt at distraction from you,
I turn to
a flock of doves
moving between the balconies.
I follow it . . . I follow it,
the flock disappears,
but you return . . .
. . . .
Only the quiet invades me,
igniting a thousand pains.
It tries to reach you,
extending a magical tongue
to erase the clamor of your presence,
erase my confusion.
It digs deep.
It digs.
It digs.
And since I've mastered hiding you,
the quiet gathers its disappointment, withdraws,
repeating,

وهو يردد
إنه اختيارك
أبقى مع صخبه وحيرتك
أبتسم له
وأردد لا أعرف
إن كان اختيارا أو انتحارا

It's your choice,
stay with his clamor and your confusion.
I smile at it,
and repeat, I don't know
if it's simple choice or submissive suicide.

كيف سنكتب عن الحب - الجزء ١
فيوليت أو الجلد - لبنان

نحن الذين فقدنا أطرافنا في حروب صغيرة!
نحن الذين تركنا الأشباح تلهو في غرفنا المعتمة
وجعلنا من النوم ملتقى لندامى الغياب!
كيف سنذهب الى الحب بأقدامنا القصيرة
نحن الذين جلسنا طويلا خلف النوافذ
ثم ارتبكنا كطَرَقات على أبواب مخلعة.
كيف سنتذوق بكل هدوء
عسل كل هؤلاء الشعراء!
نحن أبناء اللغة المُرّة،
أصحاب الندوب الغائرة
حتى آخر الموت!

How to Write of Love, Part 1
Violette Abou Jalad – Lebanon
   (co-tr. by Abeer Abdulkareem and Susan Rich)

We who lose limbs in undeclared wars,
who hear ghosts play catch in darkened rooms—
we sleep on clean sheets, mourning our past selves.

How shall we make love with these new limbs?
We who long sat aimless behind closed windows—
who lay awake confused by insistent knocking on unhinged doors.

Now we no longer taste the honeyed words
of the poets. We who still hold close the bitter language
of wars in open wounds, holding it until our final breath.

رؤوس فارغة
سوزان شكران - لبنان

يحدث أن ترمي الرؤوس في جوار منازلها وتلهو...
بعضها ماكر، بلا عطر وبلا أثر!
وبعضها لشدة إلحاحه في إثبات نفسه مُعدَّم!
وفي الحلم، سيّان!
تموت من الصقيع!
تضيع في كابوس الفراغ!
تنتهك الأقنعة!
تهلوس فقط بموجب الدفاع عن النفس!
....
رأسي في عَرَبة ودرب الهلوسة أمامي في مهبّ الريح!
وأنا أترنّح!
حسبتني استفقت لتوي من صفعة!
وإذا بي أقف على حافة حرب ووابلٍ من مطر!
كيف يجرؤ هذا الليل البغيض على توبيخي؟
كيف، وأنا منذ دهر ونيّف لا أفقه لغة الموت ولا أقتفي أثر الأشباح؟
إلامَ تؤول كلّ هذه المنبّهات؟
حتماً إلى نومٍ مبكرٍ هذه الليلة!
....
يدندن الأرق ترانيمه الخبيثة،
تبكي الوسادة...
ملّل وصمت متواطئ مع الوحشة...
عِناد يزحف كالأفعى المتململة من ضجيج فحيحها على سحابة مشبوهة!
كثيف هذا الرأس!
منتشر كالضوء...
مسموعٌ كالريح...

Empty Heads
Suzanne Chakaroun – Lebanon
(co-tr. by Julia Gettle and Mahmoud Nowara)

It so happens that heads throw themselves near their homes for fun . . .
Some of them cunning, without a scent and without a trace!
And some of them, out of extreme insistence on proving themselves . . . destitute!
And in the dream, the same!
They die from frost!
They get lost in the nightmare of emptiness!
They violate masks!
They're only hallucinating under self-defense!
. . . .
My head is in a wagon . . . and the path of hallucination is before me in the wind!
And I am reeling!
I thought I had just awoken from a slap!
And now I am standing on the brink of war and a barrage of rain!
How dare this hateful night scold me???
How, since for an eon and more I do not understand the language of death,
    and I do not follow the trail of ghosts?
To what do all these alarms point?
Surely toward an early sleep tonight!
. . . .
Insomnia hums its malicious hymns . . .
The pillow cries . . .
Boredom and silence complicit with loneliness . . .
Stubbornness crawls like a snake fidgeting from the noise of its hisses on a
    suspicious cloud!
Thick is this head!

ملموس كالخيبة...
محبّ مثلي تماماً

Spreading . . . like light . . .
Audible, like wind . . .
Palpable . . . like disappointment . . .
Loving . . . just like me
But hateful . . . like truth!

سحابة
سميرة بغدادي - العراق

أكتب على ورق الروح
لتقرأني الغابات
ويسمعني البحر
على كفي حبة قمح
وبيادر تنمو على طول الرؤى
ليس لي
غير سنبلة من عشقهم
تنظر صوب الجنوب بلهفة
وتنتظر سحابة صوتهم الأسمر

Cloud
Samira Baghdadi – Iraq
(co-tr. by Julia Gettle and Mahmoud Nowara)

I write on the papers of the soul
So the forests read me
And the sea hears me
A grain of wheat on my palm
And wheat grows along the visions
Not mine
Other than a grain of their passion
Looking toward the south eagerly
And a cloud awaits their tan voice

أربع قصائد في رثاء صديقتي!
فليحة حسن - العراق

١

مقدمة: وأما الذين نسوا عمرهم، فلهم همهم به موكلون، ولهم صمتهم به يكبرون!

كنّا

ومثل ليالٍ فقدتْ مصابيحها

نتسربل باليأس

منقسمين على أنفسنا

مخضرمو حروب

ننتقل بين "صفعات" التاريخ

دونما بارقة نصر

مدمنو منافي

نتقافز بين الشظايا

بحثاً عن قشة نعتليها

لا أرضنا لنا

ولا دماؤنا

تتأرجح أقدارنا بين أصابع الكبار

جنوبيون منشغلون بتهيئة أعمارنا للرحيل

مزاداتنا سنوات مفقوءة

وعصاً ورّثها الخريف أسماءنا

تستعمرنا الأوهام

بدلاً من الأشجار الموشية بالربيع.

Four Poems in Eulogy for My Friend!
Faleeha Hassan – Iraq
 (co-tr. by Julia Gettle and Mahmoud Nowara)

1

Introduction: And as for those who forgot their lives, they have their worries
 entrusted to them, and they have their silence through which they grow!
We were
Like nights that have lost their lamps
Cloaked in despair
Divided amongst ourselves
Veterans of wars
Moving between the "slaps" of history
Without a glimmer of victory
Addicted to exiles
Jumping between the shrapnel
Searching for a straw to hold onto
Our land is not ours
Nor our blood
Our destinies swing between the fingers of the old
Southerners are busy preparing our lives for departure
Our auctions are perforated years
And a stick that autumn bequeathed to our names
Delusions colonize us
Instead of trees embroidered by spring.

٢

أرفلُ بالحزن ممسكاً بدمي
المعلقون بأنياب الشاهدة
أصدقائي
أحتاط بجلد الماء وأنا أشير إليكم
...
مذ كان لي والد قد بيع للثكنات / السواتر
ومذ كنتُ أبالغ فيك
فأرسم كفاً أصافحها
رغم شدو السياط فوق جدراننا
- كم مرة غششتُ المعلم وقلتُ أدرس
وكنتُ أعدّ قائمة بحروفك أهيجها الروح
إيه (ميسون)
" لو كانتْ الأرض مربعة
لاختبأنا بإحدى الزوايا
ولكنها مدورة
لذا يجب أن نواجه العالم" (١)
إيه صديقتي
ما زلتُ أرفل بالحزن
ممسكاً بدمي
وما زال القصر نافذة من عظام!

٣

أجيء لأرثيك مشروعا
وقافلة من شجون
ألم تجزمي
ألا نصافح كفّ الفراق مهما استطالتْ
وتبقى أصابعنا للجذور؟
لهونا

2

I strut with sadness, holding my blood
Those hanging on the fangs of tombstones
Are my friends
I armored myself with the patience of water as I point to you
...
Since I had a father who sold to the barracks
And since I've been exaggerating about you
I draw a palm to clasp
Despite the singing of the whips over our walls
—How many times have I tricked the teacher and said I am studying
And I was preparing a list with your letters that the spirit stirred up
O Mayssoun
"If the Earth were square
We would hide in one of the corners
But it is round
So we must face the world"
O my friend
I am still strutting with sadness
Holding my blood
And the palace is still a window of bones!

3

I come to eulogize you in this project
And a caravan of sorrow
Were you not certain
That we should not clasp the palm of parting, no matter how long it may last
And keep our fingers to the roots?
Our fun

وكان الأخير
يؤثث قبراً
بشاهدة تنتحب
وينشر فوق الرمال أسمك
يقول:
إذا فار للحوت ظهراً
نخبئها فتصير الملاذ
ألم تندمي؟
أعود لانفض عنك الرحيل
وأقطع تذكرة للمجيء
تعودين
أم تراني
سأبقى أخوض الزمان
بلا نافذة؟
(ميسون حسن كمونه)
الراحلون وأدري أين وجهتم
لولا الزمان لكان القلب مأواهم
أحلك ساعة تلك التي لا أبصرُ بها بسمتكِ
تسمحين لصوتي أن يردد:
أنتِ شمس بلا غروب
وأرض بلا ضجيج
وبحر بلا دوار
أنتِ روح الأشياء!
مسرعة كأنكِ لم تبصري غير بارقة للرحيل!
بفلسفة الصمت سررتُ أيامك الصغار
فكنتِ الهدوء
وصمت الهدوء
يا جرح الموجة
فراقكِ يتآمر ضد بقائي!
الطرقات التي حفلتْ بنا
كيف أبعدني عنها؟

And it was the last

Furnishing a grave

With a tombstone sobbing

And spreading your name over the sand

Saying:

If the whale's back boils

We would hide it so it becomes a sanctuary

Don't you regret?

I come back to cleanse you of departure

And get a ticket to come

You return

Or you see me

I will keep wading through time

Without a window?

Mayssoun Hassan Kammouna

The departed and I realize their destination

Were it not for time, the heart would be their shelter

The darkest hour is the one in which I cannot see your smile

You allow my voice to echo:

You are a sun without a sunset

And a land without commotion

And a sea without vertigo

You are the soul of things!

Rushing as if you saw nothing but a glimmer of departure!

With the philosophy of silence, I wrapped your young days

And so you were the calm

And silence of the calm

O wound of the wave

Your parting conspires against my survival!

The roads that were filled with us

How did they keep me away from her?

كيف أمشي بجروح تفضحها الآه؟
ميسون
يا جنوب الشجن
لو كان حلماً نسيناه
ولكنه القدر المرتقب!

٤

وجهتُ وجهي للذي فطر السماء
فسال دم الجياع
وكان يا ما كان
(ميسون حسن كمونه)
قيل بأن حديقتهم قد ضمتْ جثتها حتى كان الفتح
وقيل بأن الاشلاء انتشرتْ
فامتلأ الرمل رحيقاً
و....
لا تاريخنا المائي
ولا قصائدهم المدهونة
قادرة على محو ظلام الأباطرة
و...
ما بين دمي والحجر النائح
أسيل أنا
...
حافر السماء بمخالب وأظافر الأرض مسنونة.
......

How do I walk with wounds exposed by moans?

Mayssoun

O south of sorrow

If it was a dream, we forgot it

But it is awaited destiny!

4

I turned my face to the one who created the sky

So the blood of the hungry flowed

And once upon a time

Mayssoun Hassan Kammouna

It was said that their garden contained her body until the conquest

And it was said that the body parts were spread

So the sand was filled with nectar

And …

Neither our watery history

Nor their painted poems

Are able to erase the darkness of the emperors

And …

Between my blood and the crying stone

I melt

…

The hoof of the sky is clawed and the nails of the earth are sharpened.

الهواء الشّحيح
فاطمة منصور - لبنان

كنت غارقة في الحلم
عندما أتاني السّيل معربدا
يخبرني عن الهواء الشّحيح
الذي يغالب رئتي الكسولة
عن متاريس الخطوط الحمراء المتاخمة
لحمم الجسد الكسير
ليشهد معي
عن جرائم الوقت الضّائع
الوقت الذي شاغلته المنافي
بالتشتّت والاغتراب
ولم تنفع معه الهدنة المشروطة
ظلّلته غمامة سوداء شاحبة
ويوما بعد يوم
تشدنا بحبالها الغليظة
تعصرنا حتى نبلغ ريق الموت
وبلا رحمة تفرّقنا مع النّحس
نواعير تدور في القضاء والقدر
آه يا وطني
إنّ الجروح لتستحي
أن تهزّ وميض حرائق الأيام المغمّضة
التي تفتح روحها على السّهولة
تضرب المقامات الرّفيعة
وتضحك بملء عرق الجبين
ودون سماح
دخلت قرّة عين الجسد.

Scarce Air
Fatima Mansour – Lebanon
   (co-tr. by Mohamed Hassan and Jennifer Jean)

I was under a slumber, in a dream
when the torrent overcame me—
told me about the scarce air
overcoming my lazy lungs,
about the red line barricades adjacent
to the lava of my broken body—
when the torrent testified to
lost time crimes—
that time tantalized by exiles,
by the dispersion and the alienation.
A conditional truce didn't work with that time
as it was obscured by a pale, by a black cloud.
And day after day,
it pulls at us with thick ropes,
squashes us until we reach the spit of death,
mercilessly separated from the jinx
by the waterwheels that spin in destiny and fate.
Oh, my homeland!
The wounds will be ashamed
to shake the shimmering fires of forgotten days
which open their spirit to ease,
strike high notes,
and laugh as fully as the sweat of the brow
that does not ask for permission.
These days are the only joy of the body.

نجاة
نسرين أكرم خوري - سوريا

أخبرتكَ أنني
لا أخشى النّحل في حضرةِ الأزهار البرّيّة
ولا أتهيّب الوقوعَ في الحبّ طالما نهايته وشيكة
لم أعد أتوجّس من أن يجرحني ورقُ الكتب الجديدة
مُذ تعلّمت كيف أمصّ نقطة الدّم عن إصبَعي قبل أن تُغرقَ وجه شخصيّةٍ يهمّ الكاتب بقتلها.
قلق التّقدم في السنّ تجاوزته بتحطيم ساعةٍ والتهام ديكٍ مشويّ.
صرتُ أكشف عن ساقيّ كلّما مررتُ بزقاق المتحرّشين
وأفتح النوافذ حين يشتدّ القصف
أعزّي القريبة بوحيدها وأنا أنفخ بالون العلكة
أشتم المتسوّلين إن لمحت الصّدق يتكسّر مع نظراتهم
وكلّما تعالى بكاءُ ابن الصديقة، قبّلتُ زوجَها.
لذا لا تستغرب حين تراني هكذا..
ممدّدةً على طاولة غسيل الموتى،
أنتظرك.

Salvation
Nesrin Ekram Khoury – Syria
   (co-tr. by Abeer Abdulkareem and Cindy Veach)

I told you
I'm not afraid of bees in the presence of wild flowers
Nor do I fear falling in love as long as the end is near.
I no longer have qualms about being cut by the page of a book.
I've learned how to suck a drop of blood from my finger before it drowns
The character about to be killed.
I've overcome fears of aging by destroying clocks and devouring grilled roosters.
I've started showing my legs when I walk down the molester's alley
And opening windows as the bombing intensifies.
I console a relative over her only child while blowing gum balloons.
I curse beggars when honesty breaks with their looks.
When the wailing of my friend's son starts up, I kiss her husband.
So, don't be surprised if you see me
Laid down on the mortuary washing table
Waiting for you.

كتابة بالماء
سميرة بغدادي - العراق

ذاكرتي في القارب المعطوب
والأمواج تبحث عن اللحظات الأخيرة
عن صدى الأمل الذي هجر المكان
عن الأمان
حين ينمو على الأشياء كالظل الطويل
أحاول مع التفاصيل الصغيرة
ألصقها في جيوب الوقت
ولو بشيء من صمغ الفرح
أحاول
وكل كتابة بالماء
تلبسني الأفق
توحدني مع ما كان من ماض
حين ابتدأت
صار الضوء يغزو أول ثقب
ويبدأ الانفصال
ليتجسد في رحم العبارة الجديدة
وأمزق انتمائي لهم
كورقة حظ خاسرة
أكسر زمنهم
كساعة جدي العتيقة
أحرر أصابعي
لتكتب الريح دون تحكم هذا القلب
أتركها
ترافق الحلم في غياهب المجهول
لتكتب طلاسم يسقيها الحلم

Writing with Water
Samira Baghdadi – Iraq
(co-tr. by Julia Gettle and Mahmoud Nowara)

My memory is in the damaged skiff

And the waves are searching for the last moments

For the echo of hope that abandoned the place

For safety

When it grows on things like a long shadow

I try, with the small details,

I stick them in pockets of time

Even with something of the glue of joy

I try

And all writing is with water

The horizon clothes me

Unites me with what was from my past

When I started

Light began to invade the first hole

And the separation starts

To be embodied in the womb of the new phrase

And I tear up my belonging to them

Like a losing lottery card

I break their time

Like my grandfather's antique watch

I free my fingers

So that the wind may write without the control of this heart

I leave it

Accompanying the dream into the depths of the unknown

To write talismans the dream will water

في خضم المستحيل
رؤيا لأمل غلبه النعاس
وغابت الحقيقة
طيف المنون

ثم يغيبون!
هكذا
وبكل بساطة يدهشهم أن تكون محزونا
وبكل لامبالاة
يتساءلون
كيف لمثل شخصك
أن يرتسم بمآقيه طيف المنون
ولما..
تبحث عن يد تمتد لك!
تبعد عن كتفيك ثقل الليل المحزون
عجبا!
متى سيفقهون؟

In the midst of the impossible
A vision of hope overcome by drowsiness
And the truth vanished
The phantom of the era

Then they vanish!
Thus
And quite simply it amazes them that you are sad
And quite indifferently
They wonder
How to, like your person
Be characterized in their eyes by the phantom of the era
And when . . .
You search for a hand to extend to you!
Distancing from your shoulders the weight of the sad night
Astonishing!
When will they understand?

ألسنة ما بعد إنخيدوانا
جاكلين سلام - سوريا

أنا، حفيدة أنخيدوانا التي تفتح نوافذ رأسها آخر المساء فيهرب الكلام كالنحل ويحط بين سطر وآخر. تقضي الليل وهي تزيح فاصلة واحدة من السطر الأول، تحذف حرف العطف من السطر الثاني، تضع شدّة على كلمة حبّ.

تفكر بأزمة اللغة العربية حين تترجم المهاجرين الجدد، وكيف يغترب العقل والقلب واللسان عن لكنة ولغة البيت الأول.

ألواحك الشعرية الأبدية يا جدة، وكتابي الالكتروني في زمن الذكاء الاصطناعي، إلى أين سيأخذنا! الموسيقى الكلاسيكية في خلفية المشهد تتسرب من رأسي إلى ظهري إلى أصابعي. الكلام لعبتي وشريكي. أخلخل قوام النص في نبضه العذري. أنسى العالم والأحبة والأعداء والذين يكرهون الشاعرات وقصيدة النثر الخارجة عن القيود.

وأنسى بكاء المرأة التي التقيتها هناك.

امرأة غريبة ترجمتُ أحزانها ساعات بعد إصابتها بانهيار عصبي.

كيف سأنسى صوت امرأة في المشفى وهي تقول: "الله يخليكم، لا تأخذوني إلى مشفى المجانين، أنا لست مجنونة، فقط يوجد طبل في رأسي، أشخاص غرباء يتكلمون...الله يخليكم ساعدوني كي أشفى وأنام...لست مجنونة.."

أحتضن أوجاع الألسنة وأحمل النقطة من رواية إلى أخرى.

أختم على ما يصدر من فمي دون توقيع اسمي الكامل:

أنا جاكلين...

ترجمانة الوردة السرية والماء،

أما زلتِ معي أيتها الجدة، إنخيدوانا

أصدقيني القول، لماذا كانوا يتهمون شهرزاد بالغاوية، حين جعلت لسانها والحكايات بديل السيف والموت؟

Words After Enheduanna
Jackleen Hanna Salam – Syria
  (co-tr. by Amir Al-Azraki and Jennifer Jean

I am a granddaughter of Enheduanna,
whose mind's windows open at dusk's last breath,
where words flee like bees
alighting between line and line.

Night passes as I shift one comma from the first line,
erase a conjunction from the second,
and put a *shadda* on the word "love."

I ponder the Arabic language predicament
when translating to English for new immigrants.
How do mind, heart, and tongue estrange
from the accent and language of the first home?

Your eternal poetic tablets, O grandmother,
and my electronic tablet in the age of AI,
where will they lead us?

Classical music in the background
seeping from my head to my spine
to my fingertips.

Words, my toys and companions,
I sway in the body of text,

in its innocent pulse.

I forget the world,
and beloveds,
and enemies,
and those who hate poets,
and the prose poem without constraints
and the tears of a woman I met there.
A strange woman, whose sorrows I translated.
A strange woman, whose sorrows I deciphered
in the aftermath of her nervous breakdown.
Can I forget that woman's voice, that hospital: *Please don't take me to the*
asylum, I'm not crazy, there's just a drum in my head, strange people speaking . . .
Please, help me heal and sleep . . . I'm not crazy!

I embrace the pain of the words and carry the burden period
from one story to another, then
I seal what flows from my mouth
Without signing my full name:
My name is Jackleen . . .
translator of the secret flower and its water.
Are you still with me, O grandmother, Enheduanna?
Tell me, why did they accuse Scheherazade of seduction
when her words replaced sword and death?

ملامح متكرّرة
سوزان شكرون - لبنان

- من أيّ جسد أقطف ذاكرة؟
الظلّ شاحب...
الرأس حزين!

- خلعت عنها ثوب الدمية ونهضت من عريها لتكتسي بالحياة...
لم تكن تعلم أنّ ثوبها الجديد، مرقّط بالعاهات/ مزيّح بالخيبة/ فضفاض على الحرية!
قالت: وداعاً
لن أعود إليّ!

- وما الجَسَد إلّا دمية تتفكك إلى قطع كل ليلة...
عندما يصحو يحاول إعادة أعضائه إلى مكانها كما كانت بالأمس!
ما عدا الرأس! يضعه جانباً، فبداخله أحلام مرتّبة يخاف عليها أن تهرب...
ثم يهرع إلى قلبه مسرعاً ليركبّه قبل أن ينهض...
فثمّة حبّ طارئ ينتظره في مثل هذا الصباح الباكر....

- ألبَسَها إحساسها بالنكران زيّاً مسموماً، كالحقد!
لا يعنيها مزيجٌ مركّب من الأدوار... كلّها سافرة!
الألوان في عالمها مريضة... كلها حيادية!
المساحات في حضورها مكشوفة... كلها عارية!
فكرة تحقيق الفراغ أهم من الفراغ نفسه كالمفهوم!
هلاميات العَدَم مشبّعة في ذاكرة موتها كالحقيقة!
عادة الحياة مملّة دون ترقيم كالخسارة!
الخشبة مُضاءة والمسرح ممتلئ كالحياة!
سيميائية اللاشيء طقس في حقل دائري كالفضاء!
اللّاهوية بطاقة فارغة في مدار الألسنية كالزمن!

Repeated Features
Suzanne Chakaroun – Lebanon
   (co-tr. by Julia Gettle and Mahmoud Nowara)

- From which body do I pluck a memory???

The shadow is pale...

The head is sad!!!

- She took off the doll dress and arose from her nakedness to put on life...

She did not know that her new dress was spotted with defects/striped with disappointment/too loose for freedom!

She said: Goodbye

I won't return to myself!

- And what is the body but a doll that falls to pieces every night...

When it wakes it tries to return its organs to their places as they were the day before!

Except for the head! It puts it aside, for inside it are sorted dreams it fears will escape...

Then quickly rushes to its heart to assemble it before it awakes...

For there is an urgent love waiting early in the morning...

- Her sense of denial dressed her in poisonous guise... like resentment!

A complex mix of roles mean nothing to her... they are all unveiled!

The colors in her world are sick... they are all objective!

The spaces in her presence are exposed... they are all naked!

The idea of realizing emptiness is more important than emptiness itself...

like the concept!

The gelatinousness of nothingness is imbued with the memory of her death...

like the truth!

Life's habit is dull without numbering... like loss!

The stage is lit and the theater is full... like life!

العرض كرويّ كالمتاهة!
صفعة واحدة تكفي لإعادة ترتيبها...
نقطة على السطر...
اكتمال!

The semiotics of nothingness is a rite on a circular field . . . like space!

Nonidentification is an empty card in the orbit of linguistics . . . like time!

The display is spherical . . . like the labyrinth!

One slap is enough to rearrange it . . .

A dot at the end of the line . . .

Completion!

مناجاة
سوزانا الحجار - سوريا

في الوجدِ بركانُ المرارةِ ما خَمَدْ
يأتي على ما ظلَّ من عقلٍ شَرَدْ
يأتي على قلبٍ تجمَّدَ فانكسر
والنارُ لم تصهَر رُكاماتِ البَرَدْ

مع كُلِّ فجرٍ يحتويني نرجسٌ
في حُضنِ دارٍ أصبحت حُلماً بَعُدْ
ويعودُ بي سِحرُ النَّسيمِ لِغرفةٍ
ذاقَت معي مُرَّ الليالي والسَهَدْ

في كُلِّ ركنٍ تستريحُ حكايةٌ
وتنامُ حالمةً أغانٍ لا تُعَدْ
وهناكَ ذاكرةٌ رفضت بأن تأتي معي
ودّعتُها والقلبُ بالهَمِّ اتَّحَدْ

لي دميةٌ بالرّوحِ أسمعُ نَوحَها
أشتاقُ حضنَكِ فالجدارُ بيَ استبدْ
ماذا أقولُ وفي الصميمِ خناجرٌ
تغتالُ ذاكرةً وعُمراً لن يَعُدْ

والغربةُ الرّعناءُ تُشعِلُ وحدتي
نارانِ تستعرانِ في بُقيةِ الجَسَدْ
يا موطناً أضناهُ هجرَ بنينه
يا نعمةَ الرحمنِ يا أوفى سَنَدْ

عُذراً حبيبي ما رحلتُ طواعيةْ
والشَّامُ أمّي والسّويداءُ الوَلَدْ
عُذراً فضيقُ العيشِ يخنقُ حُلمَنا
والحرُّ يحيا بالكرامةِ والمَجدْ

قسماً بلوعةِ غربتي وسوادِها
قسماً بدمعٍ جفَّ من ويلِ البُعدْ

Supplication
Suzannah Hani al-Hajjar – Syria
  (co-tr. by Julia Gettle and Mahmoud Nowara)

In the soul, the volcano of bitterness has not subsided
                       It comes upon what remains of a wandering mind
It comes upon a heart that has frozen then broken
                       And the fire did not melt the hailstones
With every dawn a daffodil contains me
                       In the embrace of a home that has yet become a dream
And the magic of the breeze returns me to a room
                       That tasted with me the bitterness of nights and insomnia
In every corner rests a tale
                       And it sleeps dreaming countless songs
And there is a memory that refused to come with me
                       I said goodbye to it and the heart united with concern
I have a doll with a soul whose lament I can hear
                       I miss your embrace for the wall inside me domineers
What can I say, and there are daggers at the core
                       You assassinate a memory and a lifetime that will never return
And the reckless exile ignites my loneliness
                       Two fires rage in the rest of the body
O homeland exhausted by the abandonment of its sons
                       O blessing of the most gracious, o greatest support
Apologies, my love, I did not leave voluntarily
                       And Damascus is my mother and Suwayda is the child
Apologies, the narrowness of living chokes our dream
                       And the free live with dignity and glory
I swear by the sorrow of my exile and its blackness
                       I swear with tears dried from the woe of distance

قسماً بأيامِ العذابِ وجورِها
سأعودُ نجماً في سمائِك يتَّقِدْ
يشتدُّ عودُ النَّخلِ في صحرائِهِ
والياسمينُ بدونِ شامِهِ ما صمَدْ

I swear by the days of torture and their injustice
                              I will return a star in your sky, burning
The palm tree grows stronger in its desert
                    And jasmine without its Damascus would not endure

الياسمين
سلمى حربة - العراق

كل ما نحصده ظلال شموس
تغادر عند طلعة أول نجمة درية
تعلمت ألا أتعلق بالندى
وألا أصدق عطر زهرة الياسمين الشقية
تعلمت أن أبتسم لعطرها يضوع بين أنفاس الهواء قربي
تعلمت ألا اثق بغواية الياسمين
فالبياض عالم سرمدي هائم
يجني حصاد المحبة وغواية النقاء
جنان عطر يسلب ألباب القلوب
هو حصاد الياسمين

The Jasmine Harvest
Salma Abdul Hussein al-Harba – Iraq
(co-tr. by Amir Al-Azraki and Jennifer Jean)

All we reap are
shadows of the sun
that leave after the rising
of the first shining star. I learned

not to get attached to the dew,
nor to believe in the scent
of the wayward jasmine.
I learned to smile at its scent

spreading in the wafts of the air near me—
for its whiteness is an infinite
aimless world
that reaps the harvest of love and

the temptation of purity.
The soul of its scent captivates
the heart of hearts.
It is the jasmine harvest.

قصائد
سوزان علي - سوريا

علمتني أمي كيف أغسل الإبريق جيدا
أمسكه بقلبي كي لا يسقط ويتصدع
أبدأ بجوفه المعتم
دائريا أزيل كلس الأنهار
وأتأكد في غمرة الضوء
بأن النهر مات دون جنازة
والستالستيل عاد براقا في يد العامل المهترئة
علمتني أمي غسل النسيان
دون خرقة بيضاء تلهم الريح
هنا تعيش امرأة قاسية
تعرف غسل الصحون والرفوف
نقع الخضار بالملح وخل التفاح
ولكنها
لم تتعلم كيف تجفف يديها
كيف تترك دموعها في عينيها
تعود إلى رحمها
حارة رطبة مالحة.
آه ما أطول الليل
وما أقسى حضن الأمهات
ليتني زهرة برية
ترى وجهها
في مرآة سكين.

Untitled
Souzan Ali – Syria
   (co-tr. by Julia Gettle and Mahmoud Nowara)

My mother taught me how to wash a kettle well

Hold it to my heart so it doesn't fall and crack

I start with its dark hollow

Circularly remove the rivers' limescale

And I ascertain in the depths of light

That the river had died without a funeral

The stainless steel returned shining in the worker's worn hand

My mother taught me to wash away amnesia

Without a white rag that inspires the wind

Here lives a stern woman

Who knows how to wash dishes and shelves

Soak vegetables in salt and apple cider vinegar

But she

Didn't learn how to dry her hands

How to leave her tears in her eyes

She returns to her womb

Hot, humid, salty.

Oh, how long is the night

How stern is the mothers' embrace

I wish I were a wildflower

Who sees her face

In the mirror of a knife.

أنا والأمواج
إلهام ناصر الزبيدي - العراق

إنهم أمامي
بحر
خاصمته السماء
أخذت زرقتها منه
وتركته
بحرا بلا ... لون
أمواجه ألسنة نار
تراقص رياحا
متضاربة
رقصة ماجنة
على إيقاعات
عشواء
تنفذ أعمدة دخان
تبتلع أفقا "بعيدا"
تلونه بسحبه السوداء
على شاطئ هذا البحر...
أقف
قدماي ...
جذوري انغرست برمال الشاطئ
ابتلعت حبات الرمل
وأحالتها لأرض صلبة
رأسي يتجه نحو نجمة
صافية زرقاء
تتقدم موجة ترتطم بقدمي
تتوغل جذوري أكثر...
تتقدم موجة أخرى ...
يحاول رذاذها

The Waves and I
Elham Nasser Al-Zabedy – Iraq
(co-tr. by Amir Al-Azraki and Jennifer Jean)

Before me . . . they are
ocean
argued with by the sky
who stole its blue
and left . . .
that sea without color
with waves as tongues of fire
dancing with conflicted winds,
with seductive gyrations,
to chaotic rhythms.
Pillars of smoke pierce that sky,
swallow a distant horizon
tinged with black clouds.
On the shore of this sea,
I stand.
My feet root . . .
entrench in beach sand,
digest those grains,
turn them . . . into solid ground.
My face turns toward a star,
pure and blue.
A wave crashes onto my feet,
driving my roots deeper . . .
another wave advances . . .
its spray trying
to touch my face.

أن يطال رأسي
يعلو رأسي أكثر
يعانق نجمة السماء
ويوشح لونها ...
خصلات شعري
وبريقها يملأ عيني ...
ضياء
فتبدو لؤلؤتين بيضاوين
تتحديان البحر
الذي لا لون له
وتتحديان...
سحبه السوداء
تندفع نحوي
موجة أخرى...
أزداد صلابة
وأخرى...
تزيدني إصرارا
يصرخ البحر ...
من أنت؟!
وكيف تكونين
أمام أمواجي...
جدار ا
أرد على البحر
بابتسامة
يصرخ البحر مجددا
لا تتحديني...
وتشعل ضحكتي
بين أمواجه النيران
يلملم غضبه
مكوناً موجة عارمة
تنشق عن وحش خرافي
ولد في عمق...
الماضي السحيق

My mind rises higher,
embraces the sky star,
gilding its color,
with my hair strands.
Its gleam fills my eyes,
adds radiance ...
So, they appear as pearls, ovals,
defying the sea,
the colorless sea.
And defying ...
those black clouds
rushing at me,
increasing the strength,
of another wave,
as my strength increases.
With another ...
my determination rises.
The sea screams:
Who are you?!
How can you
stand before my waves,
like a wall?
I answer:
with a smile.
The sea screams again:
Don't challenge me!
And my laughter ignites
fire amid the waves.
Gathering its rage,
forming a furious tide
unleashed from a mythical beast
born in the depths

تحمله ملايين الأرجل...
وتبرق على جسده
ملايين العيون
الحمراء
يفتح فمه عن صوت مدوٍّ ...
يكشف الفم عن...
جحيم مستعر
يتجه الوحش... نحوي ...
سكوني يبتلع... صوته المدوي
وأرجله الملايين تتكسر ... عند قدمي
وعبثا
تحاول ملايين الأذرع.....
اقتلاعي
وتفشل في
اقتلاع جذوري
أخيرا ...
تلقي الموجه بجسدها
فوقي
يحفر جسدي مكانه خلالها...
ويشقها كالسيف
إلى نصفين
تتهاوى خلفي....
على الشاطئ
أستدير ببصري...
لأرى جثة المارد
ملقاة على الأرض
ورمال الشاطئ
تنهش قطرات
الماء
تذوب الموجة
بين ذرات رمال الشاطئ
وتنطفئ ملايين
العيون الحمراء

of an ancient past,
carried by a million legs,
and on its body
a million red eyes,
the sea opens, releases a deafening roar,
revealing a blazing hellscape.
The beast moves toward me . . .
and my calmness swallows its roar.
Its million legs shatter . . . at my feet.
And in vain,
a million arms try . . .
to uproot me
but fail
to uproot me.
Finally . . .
one wave hurls its body
over me.
My body cuts through it . . .
cleaves it like a sword
into halves.
It collapses behind me . . .
on the shore.
I turn my eyes . . .
to the corpse of that monster
lying on the earth,
and the sands
as they devour drops
of water.
The wave melts
into the grains of beach sand,
ending a million
red, monster eyes.

مانيفستو الصوت والمبضع
ديمة محمود - مصر

أيتها القدّيسة الرؤوم
علميهم كيف يفتح التاريخ مصراعيْه على الصوت
وكيف تُلوّنُ الأسلاكُ اسوداد السراديب
وكيف تستيقظ السماء من آبار الصّمم
كيف ينحلُّ قوس قزح في ضبابية المشهد.
علميهم كيف يستقرُّ العالم في أصابع امرأةٍ
لِتشكّلَ منه سوناتا الصوت المفتوح بنعومةٍ إلى حافّة الخطر
ويستدير الصوتُ في مقارعة الرَّهبة
فَيلتئمُ أوّله ومنتهاه في حلقة النور واللون معاً.
علميهم كيف تولد البداياتُ في عقارب الخراب
وكيف تنضَحُ المباضع نَتَنَ الأنسجة وتضرفُ الصديدَ برقصة
وكيف لعلامات الخياطة أن تُنكَّسَ أنوف المهرّجين الحمراء
وتنفضَّ العناكب بمعطفٍ أبيض.
علميهم كيف تختصر امرأةٌ الحبَّ في مِبضعٍ
وعينين كجناحيْ نورس عائدٍ لموطنه بعد الشتاء
وصوتٍ يختصر سلّمُه كلَّ الحب والوطن والثورة
وكيف تسير الساعة عكس الاتجاه بلمسةٍ طريّةٍ من كفّي قديسة.
علميهم كيف ينعقِفُ أنف الصمت ويفغرُ فاه
وكيف يسيلُ الصمت نحو بؤرةٍ فيصير صوتاً
وأن الصوتَ فسيلةٌ من حنطةٍ وقطنٍ وعنب
وأن امرأةً من ماء ونجومٍ وقمحٍ وفضةٍ تنكأ ظَهر الصمت
وتُقصقِصُ سفح دبابةٍ لِتفصلَ منه ثوبَ عرسٍ
ليأسٍ مطعون وعيونٍ مقلوعة.
علّميهم كيف يختمرُ المِبضع في يد جراحٍ فَيلِدُ ريشةً وبالتّةَ ألوان
ويكرّسُ اللوحةَ لِصوتٍ تشير سبّابته باتجاه البياض المرقّش بالدم

Manifesto of Voice and Scalpel
Dima Mahmod – Egypt
  (co-tr. by Mohamed Hassan and Jennifer Jean)

O merciful saint,

Teach them how history opens its doors to the voice,

How wires color the blackness of tunnels,

How the sky awakens from the wells of deafness,

How a rainbow dissolves in the haze of the scene.

Teach them how the world settles in a woman's fingers,

To sculpt from it a sonata of the voice gently opened to the edge of danger,

And how the voice turns in confronting awe,

Its beginning and end merging into a circle of light and color together.

Teach them how beginnings are born in the hands of destruction,

How the scalpel drips the stench of tissues and expels pus with a dance,

How stitching marks can bow the heads of red-nosed clowns,

And shake off spiders with a white coat.

Teach them how a woman condenses love into a scalpel,

Eyes like the wings of a gull returning home after winter,

A voice that condenses its scale into all love, homeland, and revolution,

And how the clock moves backward with a tender touch from a saint's hands.

Teach them how the nose of silence hooks and yawns wide,

How silence flows toward a focal point and becomes voice,

And that the voice is a graft of wheat, cotton, and grapes,

And that a woman of water, stars, grain, and silver agitates the back of silence,

And trims the slope of a tank to tailor a wedding dress

For a stabbed despair and gouged eyes.

Teach them how the scalpel ferments in the surgeon's hand birthing a feather,
   a palette of color,

بينما يمدُّ ظهره جسراً لِموكب النبوءات والأجنّةِ والعصافير
علميهم كيف تصهرُ امرأةٌ صوتَ الثورة في قلب
وكيف تصيرُ امرأةٌ قلبَ الثورة في صوت.

Dedicating the painting to a voice whose index finger points to the white
   speckled with blood,
While extending its back as a bridge for a procession of prophecies, fetuses,
   and birds.
Teach them how a woman melts the voice of revolution in a heart,
And how a woman becomes the heart of the revolution in a voice.

ثائرة
سميرة بغدادي - العراق

جاهليتكم النكراء لم تك منصفة
تلقي بآمالي إلى برد الأرصفة
وتجرني بين السنين وحيدة
لم تبق أملا في الجوانح لأنزفه
فلتطفئوا لهب الحياة في دمي
أنتم أصحاب المذاهب المتطرفة
تعيثون في درب العقول بلا خجل
نطقتم.. ولكن بالحقيقة المحرفة
أما أنا.. فحزينة لم أزل
أتلمس الفرح علّي أعرفه
أنا.. صاحبة النبض الغريب بتفردي
لا أعتنق صوت الفرقة الخانعة
أنا.. برسن أفكاركم لم أزل
أبحث عن دليل قد تعبت لأكشفه
لي من دموع المريدين سحابة
لأعيش حلما طالما اشتقت له
لي هدف، أن أرى حريتي
ولي بعيدا عن قيودكم مستقبل لأعرفه

Revolutionary
Samira Baghdadi – Iraq
 (co-tr. by Julia Gettle and Mahmoud Nowara)

Your awful ignorance was not just
Throwing my hopes to the cold of the sidewalks
And dragging me through the years alone
There is no hope left in the wings for me to bleed
So extinguish the flame of life in my blood
You are the ones of extremist doctrines
Wreaking havoc upon the path of minds without shame
You spoke . . . but with the distorted truth
As for me . . . I am still sad
I touch joy so I may know it
I am . . . the one with the strange pulse in my uniqueness
I don't embrace the sound of the servile band
I am . . . still reined in by your thoughts
Searching for evidence that I have tried to discover
I have a cloud from the tears of the devotees
To live a dream that I have long yearned for
I have a goal, to see my freedom
And I have, far from your chains, a future to know

بومة في مهب العاصفة
سوزان علي - سوريا

خذ يا حبيبي نهدي
وأعطه لذاك السجين
ألا تسمع المطر في عينيه؟
خذ يدي وأعطها لذاك اللص
إنه يخاف الجيوب والأصابع
إنه يريد بيتا.
خذ حلمتي ومصها قرب قبر أمك
أمك مثلي
خرافة في مقام أعلى السفح
عاشت وماتت دون قبلة
رأت في شاربيك رجلا أحبته في الماضي
وعندما سمعت صوتك الخشن أول مرة
لعقت فمها كقط بري
وتفاءلت
وصبرت
وغطت زندها بضوء القمر.
أنا مثل أمك
أبحث عن جدار أتباهى بظله
أعلق عليه جسدي
وأزغرد لضعفي
لعفني
وأرقب الطحالب كيف تنتشي وتنمو
حول عيني
أرجوك ضع فرجي الذي تحب
فوق كتفك

Owl in the Middle of a Storm
Souzan Ali – Syria
   (co-tr. by Julia Gettle and Mahmoud Nowara)

Take my breast, my love

And give it to that prisoner

Can't you hear the rain in his eyes?

Take my hand and give it to that thief

He is afraid of pockets and fingers

He wants a house.

Take my teat and suck it near your mother's grave

Your mother is like me

A myth in a hilltop temple

She lived and died without a kiss

She saw in your mustache a man she loved in the past

And when she heard your rough voice for the first time

She licked her mouth like a wildcat

And she grew optimistic

And she grew patient

She covered her forearm in moonlight.

I am like your mother

I seek for a wall to boast of its shadow

I attach my body to it

I ululate to my weakness

To my rot

I watch the algae, how it rises and grows

Around my eyes

Please put my vulva that you love

Over your shoulder

كبومة شقراء
واذهب عند الغروب
إلى قبر أمك
صدقني لن تسمع بكاءها أبدا.

Like a blonde owl
And go at sunset
To your mother's grave
Believe me, you will never hear her crying.

صرخة حواء
سوزانا حجار - سوريا

أعلنتُ حدادي على شعري والصمتُ دمار..
ومشتْ في صدريَ زوبعةٌ.. تسبقُ إعصار
ماتت شفتي.. ماتت لغتي.. ودموعٌ ماتتْ في عيني..
مات الإحساسُ يناديني:
ثوري وخذي ثأر الأحرار..

ثوري كالعمرِ إذا اغتصبَ..
ثوري كالوردِ إذا احتجبَ..
ثوري كالبحرِ.. كنورِ الشّمسِ.. يُكَسَّرُ عِنْدَ الليلِ بنار..

غنّي ألحاناً تروينا..
صيغي أشعاراً تحيينا..
لا تخشي صمتاً مجنوناً.. فالصمتُ من الكلماتِ يغار..
من كان طريقُ الشمسِ رؤاهْ.. حرامٌ يقنعَ بالأمتار..

ذكّريني إحساسي المغدورِ بماضٍ من حزني ينهار..
كنتُ أضاهي الفَلَكَ عُلوّاً.. ورفاقي الأنجمَ والأقمار..
كنتُ إذا أمشي.. تخشاني جنباتُ الأرضِ وسورُ الدار..
كنتُ أغني.. أكتبُ شعراً.. وأَحَطِّمُ بالقلمِ الأفكار..
ما بالي والحزنُ طريقي...؟
واليأسُ شعاري ورفيقي...؟؟
ما بالُ القاسيةِ الحرّة.. تخشى أن تظلِمَها الأقدار....؟!!

أحببتُ الحبَّ فأضناني..
صاحبتُ العقلَ فأشقاني..

Eve's Cry
Suzannah Hani al-Hajjar – Syria
(co-tr. by Julia Gettle and Mahmoud Nowara)

I declared mourning over my poetry, and silence is destruction...
And a whirlwind walked through my chest... preceding a hurricane...
My lip died... my language died... and tears died in my eyes...
Feelings died calling to me:
Revolt and avenge the free...

Revolt like the lifetime if it was raped...
Revolt like the rose if it hid...
Revolt like the sea... like the light of the sun... broken at night by fire...

Sing melodies that narrate us...
Form poems that revive us...
Do not fear a mad silence... For silence envies words...
For whomever the path of the sun is his vision... it is forbidden to be satisfied
    with meters...

My betrayed feeling reminded me of a past of my sadness collapsing...
I was matching astronomy in height... and my companions were the stars and
    the moons...
When I walked... the ends of the earth and the walls of the house scared me...
I was singing... writing poetry... and shattering ideas with a pen...
What's the matter with me, with sadness as my path...?
And despair my motto and my companion...??
What is the matter with the stern, free woman... fearing that the fates will
    wrong her...?!!

وحلمتُ بيومٍ تحيا فيه الفرحةُ في عينين صغار....!!
سألتُ العدلَ.. وربَّ العدلِ.. سألتُ قلوباً لم تحتر..
أين الأحلامُ أربّيها حلماً حلماً حتّى تكبر...؟؟
أين البسماتُ أخبّيها لحياةٍ قد بدأت تزهر...؟؟!!

همّي يقتلني.. كلَّ صباحٍ.. كلَّ مساءٍ.. ليلَ نهار..
حزني يذبحني.. يكسر ظهري.. يرمي صبري بالأحجار..

أحتاجُ زلازلَ تقلَعُني.. تنشُلُني من حزنٍ عارم..
أحتاجُ البسمة تُنعشني.. أرهقني يأسٌ يتفاقم..
لا أدري إن كنتُ أقاومْ..
أم أني بالعمرِ أساومْ..
لا أدري إن كان كلامي.. ثورة مقهورٍ.. أم إنذار....!!

نارٌ تأسرني.. يا ويلي إذ ما حاولتُ تخطّي النار
إني مجروحٌ.. مذبوحٌ.. في صدريَ سكّينٌ قهّار..
يختالُ غروراً لا يأبهُ لو أني من ألمي أنهار
والعقلُ المسكينُ يلملمُ أشلاءً من قلبي.. تذكار..

إني إنسانٌ لستُ حجرْ..
لي حلمٌ.. إحساسٌ.. وقمرْ..
لي حقٌّ في هذي الدنيا..
والعمرُ يعاتبني لو مرْ..
لي قلبٌ يحتاجُ حناناً..
والفكرُ منَ الهمِّ تكدّر..

يا كلَّ الناسِ أجيبوني.. ما ذنبُ زهورِ الليمونِ...؟؟
هل كنتُ ضحيّةَ أفكاري.. أم فيكمْ أسرارُ شجوني....!!
أم أن فتاةً من بلدي.. عارٌ أن تسألَ أو تختار....؟!

I loved love and it exhausted me . . .
I befriended the mind and it made me miserable . . .
And I dreamed of a day when joy would be revitalized in the eyes of the small . . . !!
I asked justice . . . and the lord of justice . . . I asked hearts that were not confused . . .
Where are the dreams I raised dream by dream until they grew up . . . ??
Where are the smiles I hide for a life just beginning to blossom . . . ??!!

My concern kills me . . . every morning . . . every evening . . . day and night . . .
My sadness slaughters me . . . breaks my back . . . throws stones at my patience . . .

I need earthquakes to uproot me . . . to pull me out of overwhelming sadness . . .
I need a smile to revive me . . . I am exhausted by a worsening despair . . .
I do not know if I could resist . . .
Or if I am compromising with age . . .
I don't know if my words were . . . a revolution of the oppressed . . . or a warning!!

A fire that captures me . . . Oh woe if I did not try to jump from the fire
I am wounded . . . slaughtered . . . in my chest a conquering knife . . .
It swaggers vainly not caring if I collapsed from my pain . . .
And the poor mind picks up the pieces of my heart . . . a souvenir . . .

I am a human being, not a stone.
I have a dream . . . a feeling . . . and a moon . . .
I have a right in this world . . .
And life would blame me if it passed . . .
I have a heart needing tenderness . . .
And thought is disturbed from worry . . .

إنِّي بلسانِ نساءِ الأرضِ أنادي:
يكفينا استهتار...!!

نحنُ حضارتُكم.. غدُكُم.. ماضيكم..
نحنُ أصولُ الدنيا.. ولكم فينا.. أمٌّ.. أختٌ.. حبٌّ يحييكم..
نحنُ الحريّةُ لو رفضت أفكارٌ زائفةٌ تحميكم..

يكفيكم ظلماً يا بشراً.. عِشتُم للوهم ويا للعار..
يكفيكم ذلًّا لقيودٍ.. أكل عليها الدهر المهذار..
أطلبُ حريّة أفكارٍ لا إنكارَ الأصلِ النوّار..
حريتُنا ثورةُ إنسانٍ يرفض أخطاءَ الأمصار..
حريتُنا موقفُ إنسانٍ ضدَّ الزّيرِ بيومِ الثار..
ثُرتُم ضدَّ الوأدِ قديماً..
ووأدتمونا ونحنُ كبار...؟!

ناشدتُ عقولاً ترشدكمْ لمعانٍ بينَ الكلماتِ..
لم أكتب شعراً في يومٍ لسماعِ هديرِ الصفقاتِ..
أمنيتي أن أُسمِعَ صوتاً من ماضٍ ينزفُ للآتي..
أمنيتي أن تصغوا يوماً لحديثٍ من وجعِ فتاةِ..

فالعمرُ بأيدينا تبرٌّ..
لا ندري كيفَ أتى.. أو طارْ...!!

O all people, answer me ... what is the sin of lemon blossoms ... ??
Was I a victim of my ideas ... or do you have the secrets of my sorrows ... !!
Or for a girl from my country ... is it shameful to ask or choose ... ?!

With the tongue of the women of the earth I proclaim:
Enough disregard ... !!

We are your civilization ... your tomorrow ... your past ...
We are the origins of the world ... and you have in us ... a mother ... a sister ...
    a love that revives you ...
We are the freedom that would, if you rejected fake ideas, protect you ...

Enough injustice, O human beings ... you have lived for delusion and what a
    shame ...
Enough humiliation by restrictions left from an absurd bygone era ...
I demand freedom of thought, not a denial of the origin of lights ...
Our freedom is the revolution of a human being rejecting the mistakes of the cities ...
Our freedom is the stance of a human being against Al-Zeer on the day of revenge ...
You revolted against female infanticide long ago ...
And you killed us when we were grown ... ?!

I pleaded for minds to guide you to meanings between the words ...
I never one day wrote a poem to hear the roar of deals ...
My wish is to hear a voice from the past bleeding into the future ...
My wish is that you will listen one day to a tale from a girl's pain ...

For life in our hands is gold ...
We don't know how it came ... or flew ... !!

للعشق سترة وحذاء
سلوى بن رحومة - تونس

كان موعدنا الخامسة
دقت السادسة
ولم تأت خطاها
ولا يد سلمت
...
لِمَ لَمْ تأت؟ لَمَ أخلت بذاك الوعد
لأصبح " مالي خلق" للحب للعشق
لأحب وأفترق
أرسو على تلة الحب دون ورق
ولا أردد غير واحد هو سؤال:
لم الفراق أيتها المهزومة في حبي؟
وأظل أرتب طيفها بكل تفاصيل الحقيقة..
بالحقيبة
بضفائر الطفولة حتى امتشاق النهد
أطمئن نفسي
لعل شيئا مهمًّا أخّرها
ولسوف تأت
وفي كل مرة أعود من الموعد من نفس المكان...
أخلع سترتي العاطفية
أخلع حذاء أسفاري
أمضي حافيا من..
الحب
أمزق الذكرى بين قدمي وطين الأرض
وفي كل مرة يشتد حنيني
أعدني بأن أشد رحالي

Love's Coat and Shoes
Salwa ben Rhouma – Tunisia
   (co-tr. by Mohamed Hassan and Jennifer Jean)

Our appointment was at five,
the clock struck six,
and her steps did not come.
No hand extended in greeting.
. . .
Why didn't she come? Why break that promise?
It makes me "not in the mood" for love, for passion,
to love then part,
to moor on the hill of love without a letter,
repeating a single question:
Why separate, oh you who my love defeated?
. . . and I keep arranging her image with all the details of reality,
with the purse,
with the braids of childhood up to the budding breast.
I tell myself,
something important delayed her, perhaps,
and she will come
. . . but I return from the appointment, from the same place,
remove my coat of love,
remove my travel shoes,
walk barefoot away from . . .
Love . . .
I tear the memory between my feet and the mud,
and each time my longing intensifies,
I promise myself to pack my bags

إلى قمر آخر
إلى نقطة الصفر
لكن سترتي العاطفية لا تلبسني
ولا... يستجيب حذائـــــي

for another moon,
for square one.
But my coat of love does not fit me,
nor . . . does my shoe respond.

كيف سنكتب عن الحب- الجزء ٢
فيوليت أبو الجلد - لبنان

عادت الأشباح إلى طوافها،
الناس إلى منازلهم.
الوحشة المعلّقة في الفراغ
أرجوحة بين الحياة والموت.
رمى الله نرداً في الهوا
وكان هذا المجاز الحيّ.
رمى الشاعر نرداً في الماء
فغرقنا جميعاً في وهم الرحيل.
نحن الكائنات المتواطئة
نتدفّق في مواكب الصلاة كي نتوب عن أفراحنا.
ونصطفّ خلف البنادق كي ندافع عن صلاتنا.
في أسطورة قديمة،
رميتُ نردًا في اللغة
وكتبتُ كثيرا عن الأشباح
لكنها عادت إلى طوافها،
وها أنا في منزل مسكون بالإنس
لا تلهو به الرياح،
لا يتسكّع به الضياع، لا الضلال.
مشهد يتعثّر بالألفة والضجر
في طقس يحتاج لقفازين وقبعة،
لقبلة طويلة في الحديقة الخلفية
لجنة الله الموعودة
أو لجحيمه الافتراضي.

How to Write of Love, Part 2
Violette Abou Jalad – Lebanon
   (co-tr. by Julia Gettle and Mahmoud Nowara)

The ghosts returned to their roaming,
The people to their homes.
Solitude hanging in the void
Seesawing between life and death.
God threw a die in the air
And this was the living metaphor.
The poet threw a die in the water
So we all drowned in the illusion of departure.
We are complicit creatures
Flowing in prayer processions to repent of our celebrations.
And lining up behind rifles to defend our prayers.
In an ancient legend,
I rolled a die in the language
And wrote much about ghosts
But they returned to their roaming,
And here I am in a home haunted by humans
Where the wind does not play,
Where loss does not wander, nor misguidance.
A scene that falters with familiarity and boredom
In weather requiring gloves and a hat,
For a long kiss in the back garden
Of God's promised paradise
Or his hypothetical hell.

سائق السيارة المقتولة
سوزان علي - سوريا

_لماذا تقود هذه الجثة؟
لأنها لا تريد أن تدفن.
_ومن قتلها؟
تفجير قرب المستشفى.
_وماذا كنت تفعل هناك؟
أسعف زوجتي الحامل.
_وماذا أنجبت؟
صبيا جميلا.
_وماذا أسميته؟
كريم.
_هل يركب كريم هذه الجثة؟
نعم ويحبها أكثر مني.
_كيف عرفت ذلك؟
إنه وكل يوم يملأ ثقوبها المتفجرة بفقاعات الماء والصابون.
_ألم تخبره قصتها؟
نعم، ولكنها لم يصدقني.

The Driver of the Killed Car
Souzan Ali – Syria
 (co-tr. by Julia Gettle and Mahmoud Nowara)

—Why are you driving this corpse?
Because she doesn't want to be buried.
—And who killed her?
A bombing near the hospital.
—And what were you doing there?
Helping my pregnant wife.
—And what did she give birth to?
A beautiful boy.
—And what did you name him?
Karim.
—Is Karim riding this body?
Yes, and he loves her more than me.
—How did you know that?
Since every day he fills her exploded holes with bubbles of water and soap.
—Didn't you tell him her story?
Yes, but he didn't believe me.

تصحيح الذكريات
سوزان شكرون - لبنان

الذكريات....
لطخات مترسّبة في قعر الرأس، وتحتاج دوماً إلى تنظيف!
نقتلعها أحياناً من جذورها ونمحوها/
السبب: وجودها المربك وألمها المستيقظ عند كل احتكاك...
ننتقيها أحياناً أخرى من مراقدها ونحييها/
الهدف: مكانتها الشفافة وأثرها المداعِب للفرح عند كل اقتباس...
ليتنا نستحضرها في كل الأحيان، فقط لوجوب التصحيح!
يلزمنا دهرٌ من ورق وعمرٌ من أقلام لنعيد الصياغة من جديد...
التاريخ لا يمحِي أبداً بل يدوّن!
سجِّل:
مرّت روحي من هنا ذات شتاء...
ذاقت طعم المطر في قطرات الحلم...
تنبّهت لوجود مساء رابضٍ في حكايا العرّافات...
تَلَفَّت ذلك الرأس إلى مُناديه...
تحرّكت الذاكرة من مطرحها ومن مخدعها...
بدأت النفس بالعمل على وتيرة صباح طارئ...
اعترفْ:
ذاكرتك تستحق هذا الجسد..
احمها كي لا تهزل..
درّبها على قول الحقيقة، كي لا تخون!!!

Correcting Memories
Suzanne Chakaroun – Lebanon
(co-tr. by Julia Gettle and Mahmoud Nowara)

Memories...

Stains accumulated at the bottom of the head, and they are always in need of cleaning!

Sometimes we pull them from their roots and erase them/

The reason: their confusing presence and their pain awakening with each contact...

Other times we pick them from their graves and revive them/

The goal: their transparent place and the joyful effect of their touch with each quote...

I wish we could resurrect them every time... just for the necessity of correction!

We need an eon of paper and a lifetime of pens to rephrase it all anew...

History never erases, but records!

Note:

My soul passed by here one winter...

It tasted the rain in the drops of the dream...

It realized the existence of an evening lurking in the fortune-tellers' tales...

That head turned to who called it...

The memory moved from its place and from its bed...

The self began to work at the pace of an urgent morning...

Confess:

Your memory deserves this body...

Protect it from emaciation...

Train it to tell the truth... lest it betray!!!

يا جدتي القدس
عطاف جانم - الأردن

يا جدّتي القدس، يا مشكاةَ تكويني
إنّي عُزَيْزُكِ، صُبّي الماءَ في طيني

ولملميني إذا ما جئتُ منفرطاً
ومرهـقَ الروح من تغريبـةِ التين

وعانقيني فقلبي الآن محتشدٌ بالعشق
عتـقـتُـهُ من عهد حطيـن

فالبعدُ يا جدتي رجفٌ وزلزلةٌ
وفي جيوبكِ رَضٌّ للطوابينِ

وقلبُكِ الخيلُ تغدو في أعنّتها
تُقصقِصُ الليلَ عن سوقِ القَطّانينِ

وتمنـحُ الحُلمَ المُمْتَدَ في دمنـا
صبراً سيهزمُ بهتان الزنازيـن
....
الله يا شجرَ الغفران في قُدُسي
يهمي على الأرضِ تسبيحا وريحانا

يهمي فيخضرُ ناقوسٌ يُمَرْمِنَا
هذي البتولُ.. صباحٌ في مُحَيّانا
....

Oh, Grandma Jerusalem
Etaf Janim – Jordan
  (co-tr. by Mohamed Hassan and Jennifer Jean)

Oh, Grandma Jerusalem—the light of my being,
I am your Ezra. Pour water into my clay.

Gather me when I fall apart,
when my soul wearies of the fig diaspora.

Embrace me now as I fill with love,
aged since the time of Hattin.

Distance, oh Grandma, trembles and quakes.
In your pockets, is warmth for the mills.

Your heart, the horse that always gallops,
snips the night to reveal a market of weavers,

grants the dream that runs in our blood,
the patience that overcomes the injustice of prison.

. . . .

Oh God, how beautiful are the forgiving trees in my Jerusalem!
They cover the earth, praise God, and spread sweet basil.

They cover the earth, give life to church bells, sanctify us with Mary,
this Virgin . . . this morning in our faces.

. . . .

Oh God! Oh, trees of forgiveness in my homeland,
Alborak ascends with you and the star is baffled.

الله! يا شجرَ الغفرانِ في وطني
يعلو براقٌ به، والنجمُ حيرانُ

يعلو، كأن شهيداً ما تمخَّضَهُ
من جرحهِ شهقــةً.. والأفقُ عنوانُ
والمَرْمَيّاتُ رباتُ الصمودِ هنا
يَهزمْنَ مطرقةً.. ينهارُ سندان
....
يا جدتي، هذه الجدرانُ وانيةٌ
تمشي لِحَطَابها عِهْنًا وخيطانا

فَلْتُطْلِقي شهقاتِ الصبرِ هَيْلَلَةً
يا بؤسَ أحلامِ مِركافا وفُولْكَانا

ولْترحلوا يا اشكنــازَ الروسِ عن بــلدٍ
كان اسمــها منذُ بَدءِ الخلقِ كنعــانا

It ascends as if the martyr brought it forth

when he gasps from his wounds . . . and the horizon is a destination.

The descendants of Mary are the goddesses of defiance here.

They defeat a hammer . . . an anvil collapses.

. . . .

Oh, Grandma: these walls are vessels

offering wool and yarn.

Release the sighs of patience asking help from Allah.

Oh, misery of Vulcan and Merkava dreams!

Oh, Russian Ashkenazi! Depart the country

whose name since the beginning of creation was Canaan.

عمتو بضفيرتين تضحكان
هدى عبد القادر محمود - مصر

كبيرةٌ أنتِ يا عمتو!
تطربني العبارة ثم ألتفت لوجهي في المرآة
كلما التفت وجدت قلبي يتبعني مُضطراً
أقبض عليه مُتلبساً بالفزع الصغير
أمازحه حول فكرة التجاعيد وترهل الأثداء
هرمون الأنوثة مازال على حالته من طفولة مُتأخرة!
وكِبر لا يحضر
أعرفه لأنه سيؤكد أن فريدتي لن تحضر
وأن عمتو لن تُستبدل يوماً بــ (ماما)
أرعى صغار الرضا وأعول على السماء أن تربت خوفي
أواجه الجيوش الصغيرة المغرورة من مللي القديم
بالأغاني الممكنة والبعيدة في وقتٍ واحد
ثم أربت على ظهر قطتي المجنونة التي تتعمد تجاهل مُوائي الحزين
أنتِ كبيرة يا عمتو!
ما زالت تُسعدني هبة النسيم عند نافذة كل حافلة
عندما أحاول عناد أحبائي كواحدة لها ضفيرتين وتنورة شمسية
تضيء الساقين!
تجاعيد الوجه على الخصوص غالية وعنيدة
ترسم المرات اللانهائية للابتسام والعبوس
والنظرات المسروقة بيني وبين المحبة الساكنة
أخبو كلما سمعت البينك فلويد*
وتغريد يا ريت* يحملني على التراجع
فأضيء عتمتي الكُبرى بتذكر يد أمي
وبسمة عمتيّ
أنتظر الفجر لأصدح بدعاء خاص
تسمعنّه بامتنان
وتمدّن عيونهن لقفصي الصغير بالمفتاح
فأضحك.

البينك فلويد: فريق موسيقي شهير
يا ريت: أغنية للسيدة فيروز

Auntie with Two Laughing Braids
Hoda AbdelKader Mahmoud – Egypt
  (co-tr. by Mohamed Hassan and Jennifer Jean)

You are old, Auntie!
This phrase delights, then turns me to face the mirror.
My heart is obliged to follow, every time, and
I catch it red-handed, in a small panic.
I joke with it about the idea of wrinkles and sagging breasts.
My hormones are still the same from late childhood!
And the fact that aging does not come.
If it does, it confirms my beloved will never arrive,
and that *Auntie* will never be replaced with *Mom*.
So, I nurture youthful contentment, count on heaven to calm my fear.
I face small, arrogant armies of my ancient boredom
with tangible and distant songs, all at once.
Then pat my crazy cat who deliberately ignores my grieving.
You are old, Auntie!
I am still pleased with the buff of breezes from the window of each bus
when I try to tease loved ones as a person with two braids and a pleated skirt
that lights up my legs!
Wrinkles on my face are especially costly, relentless.
They show the endless times I've smiled and frowned,
the stolen looks between me and my beloved.
I fade whenever I hear Pink Floyd songs,
and the Fairouz song "Ya reit" (I wish!) makes me hold back.
But my vast darkness is lit with memories of my mother's hand
and the smiles of my two aunts.
I will wait for dawn to recite a special prayer,
the one they will hear with gratitude
and stretch their eyes toward, toward my little cage with the key.
Then, I'll laugh.

كيف سنكتب عن الحب - الجزء ٣
فيوليت أبو الجلد - لبنان

لم أرتدِ ثوب زفاف،
لم أخبز يديّ لأطفال،
ولا مشيت في جنازة
مع أني ارتديت السواد طويلا
لأخفي امتلائي بالكلام،
لأوهم المرآة بأني رشيقة كبيت شِعر،
طويلة كسرب حمام.
جسدي معافى من الزمن،
معفيّ من الأمومة،
من التدخين،
من المُسكرات والمنبهات،
مسكون بالأشباح،
بقصص الجان،
بالوحوش اللطيفة والذئاب الهاربة.
رأسي الجميل يحلم بموت مبكر،
بانطفاء سريع،
أن أكون وليمة للغياب،
عروسًا لدمع من أحبتهم،
قربانًا على مذبح حزنهم عليّ،
قداسًا لتنهي الملائكة جدالها العقيم
مع شياطين الكتابة،
وليرتل الحاضرون بكاءهم الطويل
على حياتي القصيرة
بـ" ليه يا بنفسج بتبهج وأنت زهر حزين!

How to Write of Love, Part 3
Violette Abou Jalad – Lebanon
   (co-tr. by Julia Gettle and Mahmoud Nowara)

I did not wear a wedding dress,

I did not bake my hands for children,

Nor did I walk in a funeral procession

Even though I long wore black

To hide my fullness of words,

To delude the mirror that I am nimble like a verse of poetry,

Tall like a flock of pigeons.

My body healed from time,

Exempt from maternity,

From smoking,

From intoxicants and stimulants,

Haunted by ghosts,

By stories of jinn,

By kind monsters and fleeing wolves.

My beautiful head dreams of an early death,

Of a quick extinguishing,

To be a feast for absence,

A bride for the tears of those I loved,

A sacrifice on the altar of their grief for me,

A mass so that the angels may end their futile debate

With the demons of writing,

And so that those present may chant their long weeping

For my short life

With "Why, o violet, are you so cheerful, when you are such a sad flower!"

رمانة
سوزان علي - سوريا

أعطاني الله كلبة شقراء
كنت أمشي قرب المنارة
صاخبة بكلام عسلي من رجل منبوذ
وكانت الريح تشق قصصها بصعوبة
وللموج حمام أزرق
مع أني لم أحلم ساعتها
وهرمونات اليقظة
اضطجعت تريد وحلا أو سردابا
كلبة رزقني بها الله
سقطت من سجن بشري لاحم
تعصر عينيها في وجهي
وتحرك ذيلها مع الأعشاب
وتقول لي
من أعلى السفح:
كوني أمي.
أسميتها رمانة
على اسم شجرة جدتي المفضلة
وانتظرت أسبوعا
كي أعلم بأنها أحبت اسمها
كلما ناديتها
خفقت كأغصان رمانة
وسقطت في قلبي.

Pomegranate
Souzan Ali – Syria
   (co-tr. by Julia Gettle and Mahmoud Nowara)

God gave me a blonde dog
I was walking near the lighthouse
Loud with honeyed words from an outcast man
And the wind was cracking its stories with difficulty
And the wave had blue doves
Although I was not dreaming at that hour
And hormones of wakefulness
Lay down wanting mud or a cellar
A dog God blessed me with
Fell from a carnivorous human prison
She squeezes her eyes in my face
And moves her tail with the grass
And she tells me
From the top of the hill:
Be my mother.
I called her Pomegranate
After the name of my grandmother's favorite tree
And I waited a week
To know that she liked her name
Whenever I called her
She waved like the branches of a pomegranate
And fell into my heart.

تفاصيل يوم عابر
خولة جاسم الناهي - العراق

كنتُ أوّد أن أُخبرك عن تفاصيل يومي:
عن شمس بلادي الدافئة في هذا التوقيت من العام!
عن خضرة الأشجار وعناقيد الثمار فيها.
عن فراشات الربيع وأزاهيره.
أود أن أحدثك عن أصوات الباعة المتجولين المارين في شارعنا،
وعن موسيقى عرباتهم وأنغام ناياتهم الحزينة!
وأسعار الطماطم
التي أصبحت عشرة كيلوات بسعر أقل من دولار
وحسرة قلبي على زارعها
وفرحتي لكونها تطعم الفقير..
أريد الحديث لك مطولا عن تفاصيل لقاءات يوم الجمعة العائلية
وشاي أمي الذي تهدره على الفحم
ودجاجها وسمكها الذي أنضجته نيران المحبة!
أرغب أيضا بالشكوى من نزلات برد نهاية العام وبداية العام الآخر
والحمى التي لم تفارقني منذ أربعة أيام.
وعن الألم الذي يتزايد في مفاصلي كلما شعرت ببعض الراحة أو الاسترخاء
هناك تفاصيل أخرى أود الخوض فيها كرائحة الغسيل في مناشره
والعطور والملابس الشفيفة في خزائنها،
وكتاباتي التي أهملتها.. وتلك الكتب التي تراكمت على طاولتي بانتظار وقت فراغ لها..
وعن تهاني بداية العام التي لا أجد وقتا للرد عليها،
وتلك الأغاني الرائعة التي أتظاهر بسماعها..
وعن فيلم لم أكمل مشاهدته خشية نهاية غير سعيدة!
تفاصيل وتفاصيل وتفاصيل
أحتفظ بها لك
لكن للأسف أنك لست موجودا!

Details of My Passing Days
Khawla Jasim Alnahi – Iraq
   (co-translated by Abeer Abdulkareem and Cindy Veach)

I want to tell you:
About warm sunshine in my country this time of year.
About the greenness of trees, how the fruit clusters
About spring's butterflies and flowers.
I want to tell you about the voices of street venders,
The music of their carriages, the sad melody of their flutes
And the price of tomatoes, less than a dollar for ten kilos,
And my heartbreak for the tomato farmers
And my joy for the poor feasting on tomatoes.
I want to talk about my family's Friday gatherings,
My mother's tea that she brews on coal
And her chicken and fish cooked with the fire of affection.
I want to complain about common colds at the end of the year
A fever that lasted four days
And the pain increasing in my joints whenever I relax.
Now, let me tell you about the laundry's spreading smell,
Perfumes and sheer clothes in my closet
And my writings that I've neglected and the books
That accumulate on my table, waiting.
And about the new year greetings I can't find time to answer
And those wonderful songs I pretend to listen to
And a movie I didn't finish for fear of an unhappy ending.
I keep these details for you though you're not there.
I wonder: Do men know they were born in our imaginations?
Before their mother gave birth to them.

أتساءل دائمًا:
هل يعرف الرجال أنهم يولدون في خيالنا
قبل أن تلدهم أمهاتهم
وقبل أن يحلم آباؤهم بوجودهم!
وأننا معشر النساء سبب وجودهم على الأرض.
لأن الله لا يرد دعاء امرأة تعشق بكل هذا الشغف!

Before their father dreamt of them.

And that we, women, are the reason for their existence.

God listens to the prayers of a woman who loves passionately.

ومضات لا حربية
هدى عبد القادر محمود - مصر

يحدث كثيرا
في مخيلتي الطفولية
يخلع بلدي قميصه الحربي
ويرتدي الفرح
وطني يا محرقة الأمل
كيف لي
بفرح أتوسله بين أيامك
ارحمني
لا تدعني
غريقا يبحث عن قرش
يتسلى بجسدي
اجتمعنا على الوجع
كعادتنا
منذ أول الحروب
نلوك أخبار الوطن
ننثر أسماء الشهداء
نبحث ببلاهة
عن صور الأماكن
التي.................
كانت
نمر على الدروب الخائفة
نعد مغادري الوطن
على الأصابع
نكتشف أنها
لا تكفي

Nonmilitary Flashes
Hoda AbdelKader Mahmoud – Egypt
   (co-tr. by Mohamed Hassan and Jennifer Jean)

It happens a lot
in my childish imagination.
My country removes its military gear
and clothes itself in happiness.

• • •

Oh, my homeland! You incinerate hope!
How can I dream
the happiness I beg to find in your days?
Have mercy!
Don't let me be
the drowning person in search of a shark
to play with my body.

• • •

We gathered around pain
as usual
since the first war,
exchanged news of the homeland,
shared names of the martyrs,
looked foolishly
for the pictures of the places
that . . .
were.
We passed the scared allies,
counted those who left
on one hand,

ونستعد لحرب قادمة
لكل حي
مجنونه
ومجنون حينا
يتساءل
أطفال جياع
أمهات ثكلى
ورجال معاقون
هكذا هي بلدان البترول؟؟؟؟
طفل جارتنا الذي صار
أباً
يتساءل
كيف هو؟؟
طعم الحياة
بدون حرب!!

and discovered all of this is

never enough.

We braced for imminent war.

• • •

Every neighborhood

has its lunatic.

Ours

is a wondering,

a starving child,

a mother who has lost her child,

a very crippled man.

Is that what an oil country looks like????

• • •

Our neighbor's child who became

a father

is wondering

what is??

What life tastes like

without a war!!

• • •

حصار
مريم سليمان - مصر

كان عقلي يقفز في كل مكان
وكنت أحاصره بمهامٍ لا تنتهي.. علّه يكف عن إزعاجي
لكن طبيبي وصف لي أقراصاً لتقوم بردعه
وشرع يحاصرني أنا بأسئلته
مهدياً لي نوعاً من البكاء لم أجربه من قبل
الأسئلة تعتصر المشاعر التي طال حبسها
يلاحقني صداها إلى بيتي
يحيط بسريري.. ويهدم سلامي
أحتمي بالفراغ الذي تصدّعت أعمدته
ألقي رأسي على أمانٍ مرهق الجناحين
ودون يدٍ أتشبث بها.. يأتي النوم محاصراً بالتعاسة

Siege
Mariam Soliman – Egypt
(co-tr. by Julia Gettle and Mahmoud Nowara)

My mind was jumping everywhere
And I was besieging it with endless tasks . . . such that it would stop tormenting me
But my doctor prescribed me pills to deter it
And he proceeded to besiege me with his questions
Bequeathing me a type of crying I had never experienced before
The questions squeeze out feelings that have long been trapped
Their echo follows me home
Surrounds my bed . . . and destroys my peace
I take cover in the void whose columns have cracked
I lay my head upon safety with exhausted wings
And without a hand to hold onto . . . sleep comes besieged by misery

مياه مشبوهة
منى العاصي - فلسطين

خرجت من عيادة طبيبي، خفيفة كمغفرة
تركت في حوض أسماكه رجالا كانوا يسبحون في دمي.
علّقت على جدران عيادته، الصور المبعثرة في ذاكرة مصباحي. حتى الأسماء، التي كان يلقيها الأصدقاء تحت نافذتي كحبات قمح يابسة، زرعتها له في أصيص حبقته.
أصطاد كل النحل من قميصي وأنظف ألوانه المائعة من الحدائق
أنا خفيفة من قصائدي أغرقتها في كأس البيرة،
ومن أصدقاء كانوا يزدحمون في قلبي بلا أكتاف.
خفيفة من عصافير كانت تعشش في جديلة قلبي
خفيفة كوعد الغواية،
خفيفة إذاً من رجالي ومن أصدقائي،
من صوري ومن ملابسي،
من نصوصي ومن نافذتي التطل على عجوز تكتب رسائل لله عن وحدتي
أنا
خ
ف
ي
ف
ة
سوى من اسم تسيل منه امرأة يابسة

Mirage
Muna Alaasi – Palestine
   (co-tr. by Dima AlBasha and Jennifer Jean)

I left my doctor's clinic—weightless with forgiveness.

In his fish tank, I left men swimming in my blood.
On the clinic walls, I hung photos scattered in the lantern light of my memory.
The names recited by friends under my window,
like dried wheat seeds—I planted in his basil pots.
I hunt all the bees from my shirt & I clean the colors that melt over gardens.
Every poem sinks in my glass of beer, & I'm light
of friends that crowded my heart without shoulders,

of friends that nested in my heart braids.
Lightness is a tempting false promise.
So—I'm not weighted by my men & my friends,
by my clothes & my photos,

by my writings & my window framing an old woman writing to God about
   my loneliness.
I am

أنا
خ
ف
ي
ف
ة

Except for the weeping of the name: *dry woman*.

   * The letters in Arabic spell out khafifah which means weightless or light.

ظلك الذي يُشبهني
هدى عبد القادر محمود - مصر

أعجز عن الرؤية..
لكنني أشعر بك تلدني كل مرة
تلمسني كرحم يُغذي ما بقي مني عندك
تزرعني كل مرة
لتحصدني بكلمة واحدة
هذا الضعف اللذيذ، العجز المُحبب
شعوري بالانطواء تحت جناحك، عندما تجذبني
عندما تدفعني نحو الفراغ
الغضب المُفتعل لأحصل على حريتي!
لا دار للعجزة يمكنها إيوائي الآن يا صديقي
مقعدي المتحرك الذي تدفعه يذهب أبعد مني
في طرقات باردة ... دونك
أنت طيب وعذب كعاصفة على وشك الجنون!
حتى أنني أحببت اقتلاعي من نفسي لأجلك
فقط لتُكرر: "ليس هكذا.. انظري يمكننا البدء من جديد"
كبيرٌ أنت كما تريد
لكنني كظلك لا يُعجزني حجمك
إنه فقط النور ما يُخرجني منك
تُغمض عينيك..
فأتلاشى.

Your Shadow Which Looks Like Me
Hoda AbdelKader Mahmoud – Egypt
(co-tr. by Mohamed Hassan and Jennifer Jean)

I can't see clearly,
but I feel you birth me every time
you touch me, like a womb feeding what's left of me with all of you.
You root me every time
then reap me with one word.
This is delicious weakness, loving helplessness,
this shyness under your wing when you yank me,
when you shove me into a void—
into *faux* anger to gain freedom!
No hospice can house me now, my friend.
The wheelchair you push me in moves far, far, beyond even me.
Down cold paths . . . without you!
You're nice and delightful like a storm on the verge of insanity!
I even love to uproot myself for you,
just so you repeat: "Not like this . . . Look, we can start over."
You're as big as you wish to be,
but like your shadow, I am not disabled by your size.
Only the light will remove me from you.
When you close your eyes . . .
I disappear.

قُدامى المجاهداتِ
حنان حداد - الأردن

فوالَّذي وَضَعَ النَّابِضَ بَينَ الأَضلُعِ في أيسَرِ صَدري

وَالَّذي مَلأَهُ بالقَاني وأجرَاهُ في أوردَةِ عُروقي وشرياني

لَو أمضيتُ عُمراً فَوقَ عُمري سَاجِداً على ركابَاتي

ومَلأَت كُؤوسَكِ بِحُورَ حُبٍّ وَفاضَت شوقاً بعَبراتي

لَما أوفيتَك بَعضاً مِن فَيضِ محرابِ عَينَيكِ لِمُداواتي

مَن مُثلِكِ طَالَت لَياليهُ نَاصِتاً لِبُكَائي وشكوى صرخاتي

كُنتِ وما زُلتِ ذَلِكَ المَرهَمُ الشَّافي عِلاجًا لجُراحَاتي

ذاكَ الَّذي عَجِزَ عن مُداواةِ أخاديد في كَفَّيكِ الجَميلات

وَخُطوطاً حفرَها الزَّمَنُ في الوَجنَاتِ لتَتَورّد وَجنَاتي

شَبابُ عُمرٍ ذَوى ومَضَى بِهِ العُمرُ ليزهرَ شَبابي

وَمَفَارِقُ رَأسٍ تَلوَّنَت بِغُبارِ زَمَنٍ لا يَرحَمُ جداً قَاسي

وَظَهرٌ حَناهُ دَهرٌ بِعَجلَةٍ مِن أمرِهِ سَائرٌ وأمٌّ تُعاني

تَعِبتِ وسَهِرتِ وعَانَيتِ وجُلَّ ما قَاسَيتِهِ لمجَاراتي

فَيا زَمَناً كُن رَحيماً عَلى مَن سَكَنَت رُوحي

The Veteran Strugglers
Hannan Haddad – Jordan
   (co-tr. by Julia Gettle and Mahmoud Nowara)

I swear by the one who placed the spring between the ribs on the left side of
   my chest
And the one who filled it with crimson and circulated it in my veins
And my arteries
If I spent a lifetime beyond my lifetime prostrate upon
My knees
And your cups were filled with seas of love and overflowing with yearning
For my tears
I wouldn't repay you with some of the overflow of your eyes' mihrab
To heal me
For those like you, nights stretch listening to my weeping and screams' complaints
You were and you remain that healing ointment, a treatment
For my wounds
The one who couldn't heal the grooves in your palms
The beautiful ones
And lines carved by time to blush
My cheeks
The youth of a lifetime has withered and age passed to blossom
My youth
And a head's intersections were colored with the dust of a very unforgiving time
Harsh
And a back bent by an eon with all due speed, and a mother
Suffers
You tired and stayed up late and suffered and most of what you endured was
To keep up with me

وَوِجداني
واستولَتْ عـلى العَـقلِ مِني وصَوتُها مِـن أعظَم أمنياتي
مَغروسَةٌ أُمي كَشَجَـرِ الحُورِ في قلبي مُنذُ غَـابِـرِ أزماني
مَنْ مِثلُها لَـهُم الجَــنة فَـهي مِـثلَ قُدامى المجاهداتِ

So, o time, be merciful to the one on whom dwells my soul

And my sentiments

She seized from me control of the mind and protected it from the greatest

Of my hopes

My mother was planted like a poplar tree in my heart since ancient

Times

Those like her will have Paradise, for she is like the veteran

Strugglers

الفقد
نسرين أكرم خوري - سوريا

الفَقد جعلها أُمًّا أكثر ممّا يجب،
جعلها أُمًّا بشكلٍ لا يطاق.
في بداية اليوم الثامن والعشرين من كلّ شهرٍ
تمرّر يدها برفقٍ على بطنها
كما لو أنّها تمسح دمعةً عن خدّ بَتلة
تنظّف خزانتها من السّجائر وقناني البيرة والجينزات الضيقة والهواجس
تنام على جنبها الأيسر
وتنتظر..
في نهاية اليوم الثامن والعشرين
تعاود نحيبها
تسقي فقدها كما يليق بوردة
تحتفظ بأشواكها عميقًا في قلبها
بينما الدماء تسيل بالقرب.

The Loss
Nesrin Ekram Khoury – Syria
   (co-tr. by Abeer Abdulkareem and Martha Collins)

The loss made her a mother
Made her a mother in an impossible way

At the start of the 28th day of each month
She gently pats her belly
As if wiping a tear from a petal
She cleans her closet of cigarettes, beer bottles, tight jeans, fears
She sleeps on her left side
And waits . . .

At the end of the 28th day
She cries again
Watering her loss as it were a flower
Keeping its thorns deep in her heart
While blood flows nearby

لم ألدها
هدى الدغفق - السعودية

تحاكمني
باسمها
عائلة
لا تشاء
أن أكتب،

لم أكن ذكراً
لتفخر بي،
عائلةٌ لم ألدها
لا تستحقني
ليتني
ابنةُ
أفكاري
تُعلمني
اللغات كلها
أعزف موسيقى موزارت
أغني أغنيات فيروز
أرقص مثل كل فراشة
أسبح مثل أية حورية
أركب الخيل
أتزلج حريتي
أرتحل من بلاد إلى أخرى
أكمل دراساتي خارج حدود الخريطة
أكتب ما أشاء
أجهر بأشعاري الثائرة.

I Did Not Give Birth to It
Huda Aldaghfag – Saudi Arabia
 (co-tr. by Mohamed Hassan and Jennifer Jean)

They prosecute me,
in their name,
the family name
that does not want me
to write.
I was not a male
so the name was not proud,
so the family I did not birth
does not deserve me.
And, I wish I am
a daughter
of thoughts
teaching me
every language.
I want to play Mozart,
sing Fairuz,
dance like butterflies,
swim like nymphs,
ride horses,
skate to freedom,
from country to country,
completing studies outside borders,
writing whatever I want,
loud with poems of fury,
without censorship,

دون رقابة
دون موروث
دون مجتمع يهدرني.

ذاتي
شاعرة
أغوي
شياطينها
ترى
ملائكتي
أختبئ
تحت جناحها
ذاتي التي
تفتخر بي
لأنني
أنثى
سأنتسب إليها.

without tradition,
without a society wasting me.
I am
a Poet
enticing
my demons,
observing
my angels,
hiding
under poetry's wing.
I am a self
proud of me
because I am
a female.
And she is my family.

دعنا معاً
هناء أحمد - العراق

نتقاسم حرمان الوطن
وتُصلب أحلامنا على الأسلاك الشائكة
تتقاسمنا شاشات التلفزة وأنامل الكتّاب
وتهرول القبور مسرعةً إلينا ...
...

دعنا معاً
كطفلين يقهقهان
بجيوب مملوءة ببالونات وأقلام كرتون
وأعياد تمتد إلى آخر الأحلام ...
...

دعنا معاً
نحلم بالتأرجح على الهلال
ونعيش لحظة قصيرة نتجاهل فيها تمثال الحرية..
...

دعنا معاً
نتصنع الدهشة
لفرار هذا الوطن من كتب الجغرافية المدرسية
...

دعنا معاً
نرتدي أكبر ابتسامة من نخيل
لربما لربما
نفاجأ ذات يوم
تلفّنا أحضانه
ويقسم بيننا
رغيف حنانه ... وبراميل اللبن ...

Let Us—Together
Hanaa Ahmed Jabr – Iraq
(co-tr. by Dima AlBasha and Jennifer Jean)

—share the forbidden homeland
as our dreams are crucified on barbed fences,
on TV, & by novelists—
as our graves rush toward us ...
Let us—together
—laugh like two kids with pockets full
of uninflated balloons & cartoon scribbles—
the souvenirs of holidays that last
as long as the dream lasts ...
Let us—together
—dream of swinging on a crescent
moon, of living in a moment
where we ignore the statues of liberty ...
Let us—together
—pretend we're surprised
Iraq has abandoned a schoolbook geography ...
Let us—together
—adorn ourselves with a date palm smile
so that maybe (maybe!) we're surprised one day
when this country holds us close—
let us taste—together
—its loaf of tenderness,
its barrel of buttermilk.

نساء من مطر وحرير
ماجدة الظاهري - تونس

كنا أوثقنا حلمنا لسارية مركب
على حافة البحر
لم نكن غير أشرعة
تستعد لعناد الريح حين ثار فينا
كل هذا الموج صار موسيقى
دعونا البحارة للرقص
راقصنا معهم الريح
حتى سكن البحر قليلا
الجهات كثيرة
والبوصلة أشارت لنا
بليل يقيس خطواتنا بحبات المطر
البحارة يستغربون من ليل نساء
من مطر وحرير
خفيفات ينزلن
مع مطر يهطل على غابة من كلام
لم نؤذ البحر
لم نؤذ البحارة
لم نؤذ ليل المدينة المؤرقة بالحلم
لم نخرج أحدا من الجنة
صنعنا قمرا لهذا الليل
نبراسا للهاربين من العتمة

Women of Rain and Silk
Mejda Dhahri – Tunisia
  (co-tr. by Mohamed Hassan and Jennifer Jean)

We tied our dream to the mast of a ship
on the edge of the sea.
We were nothing but sails
preparing for the stubborn wind when it blew within us.
All these waves became music.
We invited the sailors to dance.
Together, we danced with the wind
until the sea calmed a little,
the route varied,
and the compass pointed us toward
a night that measured our steps with raindrops.
The sailors were amazed by a night of women
of rain and silk.
Light descended, then,
and rain fell on a forest of words.
We did not harm the sea.
The sailors were not harmed.
We didn't harm the night of a city tormented by dreams.
We didn't expel anyone from paradise.
We made a moon for this night,
a beacon for those fleeing darkness.

ذُهان المُدُن
سوزان شكرون - لبنان

في صباحٍ مضطرب، استفاقت بعض المُدُن على حالةِ إعياءٍ عاطفيّ مصحوبة بعاصفةِ هذيان!
كلّ المؤشرات كانت تدلّ على وقوع ثورة، إلّا أنّ الفوضى المبعثرة في المكان أدّت إلى انفصامها!
مَشَت على درب الهلوسة وهي تبحث في وجوهِ المارّين عن أنقاضها!
لم تعد قادرة على التمييز بين واقع وجودها ووهم الفضاء المنتشر في خيالها!
دخلت في ارتيابها إلى منزل الجنون، وصارت تُحاكي هيجانها بمفرداتٍ مشربكة!
أخفقت في علاجها، ولم تستجب للعقاقير المضادّة للوهن!
جَلَست متراخية على أريكة الذكرى لتستريح، فبدأ الماضي باجترار خياباتها!
لشدّة آلامها غَفَت...
وفي الحُلُم، راودتها قصص الأطفال وحكايا العرّافين، فشرعت ترسم بيوتهم!
إنّها مُدُنٌ مصابةٌ بالذُهان!

The Cities' Psychosis
Suzanne Chakaroun – Lebanon
(co-tr. by Julia Gettle and Mahmoud Nowara)

In a turbulent morning, some cities woke up in a state of emotional distress accompanied by a delirious storm!
All signs were pointing to a revolution occurring, except that the chaos scattered through the place led to its
> disintegration!

She walked the path of hallucination while seeking her ruins in the faces of passers-by!
She could no longer distinguish between the reality of her existence and the illusion of the spreading space in her
> imagination!

In her uncertainty she entered the madhouse, and she began embodying her rage with confusing vocabulary!
I failed to treat her, and she did not respond to the antiasthenic drugs!
She sat slouched on the couch of memories to rest . . . so the past began to ruminate on her disappointments!
She slept from the severity of her pain . . .
And in her dream . . . she recalled children's stories and fortune tellers' tales . . . so she decided to draw their houses!
These are cities plagued with psychosis!

بنات الشمس
ليلى السيد - البحرين

الرصاصة كانت تدرك طريقها جيدا
إلى قلب شهيدة في قلب الميدان
إلى قلب الفكرة في البيان
إلى مجاز القصيدة في الديوان
أبكيك وتبكي معي
سيدة في العراق تباع بالمزاد
يشد وثاقها شيخ
كلما هم برفع جلبابه
تعالت الصيحات
تكبييييييييييييير
أبكيك وتبكي معي
سيدة في الشام تجمد دمعها
تلتقطه حبة حبة
تطهوه الليلة عشاء لأحبتها
قبل أوان موعدها
لفض باب الجنة لسيدها
كلما فتل لحيته طويلا
علا جلبابه كثيرا
تتعالى الصيحات
تكبييييييييييييير
أبكيك وتبكي معي
شابات جميلات
أجمل من بساتين الورد
ترتعد أوصال السجان كلما
ضحكن للشمس

Daughters of the Sun
Mejda Dhahri – Tunisia
(co-tr. by Mohamed Hassan and Jennifer Jean)

The bullet knows the path
to the heart of a martyr in the center of the square,
to the heart of an idea in a well-known phrase,
to the metaphor in the poem in the collection.
I cry for you and you cry with me
for a woman in Iraq sold at auction,
her bonds tightened by an old man
each time he lifts his robe—
and everybody cheers:
Takbir!
I cry for you and you cry with me
for a woman in Damascus whose tears freeze.
She collects them, drop by drop,
cooks them tonight for dinner for her loved ones
before the time comes
for her to break open the gates of paradise for her lord.
Every time he twists his beard, slowly,
his robe rises, often—
and everybody cheers:
Takbir!
I cry for you and you cry with me
for beautiful young women
more beautiful than rose gardens.
The jailer trembles whenever
these beauties laugh at the sun,

وكلما دست الشمس شعاعا
في وجه حرة وفي وجوه رفيقاتها
أبكيك وتبكي معي
هناك في سجون الاحتلال
ملاك
ملاك فلسطينية لم تكبر بعد
ملاك تحلم بلعبة وكتاب
ملاك تريد بلادا
ملاك تربك أمن الاحتلال
يضرب الشيخ صدره
"السجن للرجال"
تتعالى الصيحات
تكبييييييييييييييير
أبكيك وتبكي معي
سيدة في كوباني
كلما بكى وليدها
شدت على الزناد
أصابت طلقتها عين السواد
فدر الصدر حليبا للبلاد
أبكيك وتبكي معي
تونسيات
يرتبن للخطو مسيره
بنات الشمس
للحرية عنوان وحيد
بلاد لا ترفرف فيها رايات السواد
غنوا جميعا بدون
تكبييييييييييييييير
يحيا الإنسان

whenever the sun presses a ray

against the face of a free woman and her companions.

I cry for you and you cry with me.

There, in the prisons of the occupation, is

an angel,

a Palestinian angel not yet grown,

an angel who dreams of a toy and a book,

an angel who wants a homeland,

an angel who confounds the security of the occupation.

The old man beats his chest:

Prison is for men.

And, the cheers escalate:

Takbir!

I cry for you and you cry with me

for a woman in Kobani.

Whenever her child cries,

she prepares to pull the trigger.

Her shot hits the eye of darkness,

and the milk in her breasts flows for the nation.

I cry for you and you cry with me

for Tunisian women,

who prepare for a march,

Daughters of the Sun.

There is only one address for freedom:

countries where no flags of blackness flutter,

all of you, sing without

Takbir

and long live humanity!

بدون عنوان
فيوليت أبو الجلد - لبنان

لم أخبئ للغيب ذهبا
لا ولدا، لا عشقا
صرفتُ ما في الجيب على الألعاب النارية،
على الطائرات الورقية
أنفقت قلبي في دكاكين الورد،
في محال الأغاني،
الشريط يدور
حياتي تدور
كنت الآه العالقة في حنجرة المغني،
كنت آخ الدامعين من هول الموسيقى
لم أترك للغد بخشيشا
ولا سددت للتاريخ أقساط عمري

Untitled
Violette Abou Jalad – Lebanon
 (co-tr. by Amir Al-Azraki and Jennifer Jean)

I didn't save gold for the unseen future.
Not for son, nor for lover.
I spent pocket change on fireworks,
on kites.
I spent my heart in florist stores,
in music stores.
As a cassette tape spins,
my life spins.
I'm the lingering *Ah*
in a vocalist's throat—I'm the weeping
Ah of melody.
I didn't leave a tip for tomorrow,
I didn't pay the premiums of my age.

انتصار
هدى عبد القادر محمود - مصر

اليوم قررت نسيانك
لم ألق
عليك
تحية الصباح
تجاهلت بريدي
كي لا أستلم
زهرة القداح الصباحية
و فنجان قهوتي يتيم
لم أفكر بإعداد
طبق الطعام الذي تتلذذ به
لم أكتب لك أو...... عنك
تجنبت النظر
إلى هاتفي
تجاهلت متابعة برنامجك المفضل
وعند العصر انشغلت
بزهوري الباكية
لكن الغروب....
كسر قراري
والليل......
شرع جميع أبوابه لك
ليعلن
انتصارك
على يومي

Victory
Hoda AbdelKader Mahmoud – Egypt
(co-tr. by Mohamed Hassan and Jennifer Jean)

Today, I decided to forget you.
I did not say
good morning
to you.
I ignored my mail
to avoid receiving
the morning orange blossom.
My cup of coffee is an orphan.
I did not think to prepare
the dish that you savor.
I did not write to you . . . or about you.
I avoided glancing
at my phone.
I ignored your favorite show.
Late afternoon, I got busy
with my weeping flowers.
. . . Nevertheless, the sunset
fractured my decision.
And the night . . .
opened all its doors to you
announcing
your victory
over my day.

نصف.. وأشياء أخرى
هدى المبارك - السعودية

يحبونني بيضاء البشرة،

ساذجة، جسماً ضئيلا،

ذيل حصان تسجد الريح أمامه!

قابلة للسير مع القطيع،

وأن أتبجّح أن الموت لا يأخذ إلا الملائكة من البشر،

نصف وجه،

نصف نضج،

نصف براءة،

نصف شاعرة،

ترى الخيوط المجمعة لأشلاء قلبها تتساقط، أمام نطفة الشعر!

أعرفني جيدا، يعرفونني بأنصاف حقائق،

أربعة أحرف يسبقون بها اسمي من باب التكلف،

ومن باب الجهل، يثقبون كل جميل بيّ

يحبونني أن أنسل تحت الظل،

وأن أمشط الليل لرجل لا يفهم صمتي، لا يعي كلامي.

يحبونني المرأة المطيعة جدا،

الموافقة لوأد إحدى أنصافي بالأخرى،

ليرغبوا بكل جميل لا يروه،

سمراء،

شعر مموج،

فاشلة بالحب مصادفة!

لا يحبوني وأنا..

صفراء،

مزاج عكر،

حبلى بالقصيدة.

Half... and Other Things
Huda Almubark – Saudi Arabia
(co-tr. by Abeer Abdulkareem and Danielle Pieratti)

They like me fair-skinned,
small-bodied, naïve.
Open to moving with the herd,
like a horse tail the wind kneels before!
They brag death only takes the angels among us—
half-faced,
half-grown,
half-innocent.
The half-poet,
who sees her heart's gathered threads falling before the seed of a poem!
Know me well, reader, though they know me through half-facts,
preface my name with four letters out of courtesy,
and pierce, in their ignorance, every beauty in me.
They like me to sneak in shadow,
combing the night for a man who perceives not my silence nor my speech.
They like me obedient,
approving the quash of one half by the other,
and desire every beauty they cannot see—
brunette,
curly-haired,
failing in love accidentally!
They don't love me and I...
am pale,
of foul mood,
conceiving the poem.

شرقيةُ الهَوى
حنان حداد - الأردن

شَرقيَّةُ الـهَوى أمَلي وَحَياتي وقَلبي تَصَدَّرت

بنسـائـمِ الـرَبيـعِ وعَطـرِ ورُودهِ تَعطَّرَتْ

بخـيوطِ الـشَّمسِ حُمـرُ وجَناتِها تَوردَت

بخَافِتِ ضِلِّ القَمَرِ عُيونُها تَكحَّلَت وتَجمَّلتْ

قَصَائدُ حُبٍّ وأشعارُ غَزلٍ بجَمالِها دُوِّنَتْ

تَباهَتْ شَرقيَّةُ الهَوى بزَهرِ شبابها فتدللت

وبزَهـوِ شبابِها سُوادُ عَينَيها بيَّ تَجَبَرتْ.

Eastern Passion
Hannan Haddad – Jordan
 (co-tr. by Julia Gettle and Mahmoud Nowara)

She of eastern passion is my hope and my life and my heart
She took the lead
With spring breezes and the perfume of its roses
She perfumed herself
With the filaments of the sun, the redness of her cheeks
She blushed
With the softness of the shadow of the moon, she lined her eyes
And made herself beautiful
Love poems and courtship verses to her beauty
Were written down
She of eastern passion boasted of the blossoming of her youth
And grew pampered
And with the vanity of her youth her eyes blackened to me
She grew arrogant

تعاريف
نادية الخطيب - العراق

قلبي
كمثرى
لن يتسعَ لها جيبُك
وقلبي.. فاكهة
يفسدها
سوء التخزين

الحكاية
طفلة
لا تقودها البراءةُ
إلى مدينةِ الملاهي

كلما ارتفعَ
منسوبُ الصدقِ
في الحكاية
غرقَ الفرحُ

كلُّ لقاءاتنا
مؤرَّخةٌ
حتى ما انتهى منها
بمديةٍ في ظهرِ الحكايةِ
عندما لا تهرولُ قدمي
في باحةِ دربِك
أُدركُ
أنَّ الموتَ
تسلقَ جسدَ الحكايةْ

Definitions
Nadia Al-Katib – Iraq
   (co-tr. by Amira Al-Azraki and Jennifer Jean)

My heart is a pear
your pocket can't contain—
my heart is poorly

stored. It starts to rot.
My story? I'm a girl
tempted into

a wonderland.
The more truth I know
here, the less joy

I know
everywhere. Our meetings
are marked by the knife

of the past.
And, my feet can't run
in your gorgeous garden—

where death
overtakes the body of
my story. Should I repair

هل كان عليّ
أنْ أُرمّمَ جناحيك
لتطيرَ بهما
خارج الحكايةِ؟

your wings for you?
To fly?
Out of this love

story?

أغطية العفن
ليلى السيد - البحرين

أيتها الروح من أي عفن تهربين،
وما من جسور لفرح؟
تراجعت أغطيةُ الحب،
تراجعت حكايا الحوريات،
وكثرت رحلاتُ الموتى.
العفن مسكَ البحرَ
فرفعَ أشرعةَ السواد،
يدورُ في الموانئ
وليسَ ثمة أحدٌ
يفكُّ عن القدرِ البلاءَ.
ما جدوى صراخي
والأرضُ
قد هجرت الترابَ
فالناطحاتُ، الغاضبات، الراقيات، الراسيات
تحميك من عفنِ الغبار
من عفنِ الثياب في صحن يومك
من هزِّ جذع الحسرة
فتتساقط نشرة العفن.
احمِنا...
مازال حبُّنا ضريراً،
واللونُ عندَه
قد خالطَ الرمادَ والسوادَ.
سترفع كأسَك
في صحةِ النجوم والرفاقِ
تسقطُ في الطريق.

Covers of Rottenness
Layla Al Sayed – Bahrain
   (co-tr. by Mohamed Hassan and Jennifer Jean)

Oh soul, from which rottenness do you flee,
where there are no bridges to joy?
The covers of love receded,
the tales of nymphs receded,
and the journey of the dead multiplied.
Rottenness seized the sea,
and raised the sails of darkness.
It roams the ports,
and there is no one
to relieve fate of this affliction.
How futile is my screaming,
when the earth
has abandoned the soil?
The skyscrapers, the angry, the elegant, the steadfast,
protect you from the rottenness of dust,
from the rottenness of clothes, in your day's dish,
from shaking the trunk of regret
so that the leaflet of rottenness falls.
Oh, protect us . . .
our love is still blind,
its color
has mixed with ash and darkness.
You will raise your cup,
with cheers to stars and comrades,
you will fall along the way.
Knock on a door to be greeted by rottenness

اطرق باباً ليصافحَك العفنُ
في ثقبِ الكلمات.
الخذلانُ أنيابُ الأفكار القادمة.
اقرأ شعراً
سيصلُك النباحُ المبتهجُ
زهرةً متعفنةً
في أواخرِ ربيعٍ عفنٍ.
أعماقُنا متوحشةٌ.
لذا لن تطبخ
ربيعاً طازجاً
ستزكم أنفَك رائحةُ
طحينٍ عفن.

أيادي الماضي
ترقصُ رقصةَ سيوفٍ عفنةٍ،
اسفلتٌ مبلولٌ بدم.
قاوم العفن،
اعتصموا بالدم،
وللدم كرهوا الجسد،
ينحبس المللُ في دواخِلنا
فيتعفن.
نحن نذبل
نفقد أهليتَنا للعيشِ
في المكان،
نحاولُ،
نفقدُ البريق.
نحن نرفضُ الهرمَ،
نرفض الامتداد،
كعادتنا في الرفض،
الجحود.
الوقت لا يفزعُنا

in the crevice of words.
Betrayal is the fang of forthcoming ideas.
Read poetry,
and the joyful barking will reach you,
a rotten flower
at the end of a rotten spring.
Our depths are wild,
so you won't cook
a fresh spring.
You'll be choked by the smell
of rotten flour.
As the hands of the past
sway in a dance of rotten swords,
asphalt soaked in blood,
resist rottenness,
hold fast with blood.
And for this blood, they'll hate the body.
Boredom is trapped inside us,
and it rots.
We wither,
We lose our fitness to live,
in place.
We try,
but lose the sparkle.
We refuse to age,
we refuse to extend,
as usual, in our rejection,
and ungratefulness.
Time does not scare us.
Only the trees
understand autumn,

الأشجارُ وحدها
تدركُ الخريف،
تتركه ينحدرُ في لونِها.
تتحملُ سقوطَ أوراقِها،
فلا تتعفن.
تستيقظُ بأغصانٍ
تعشقُ تمدُّدَها.
نحن نرفضُ الهرم.
نرفضُ الامتدادَ.
كعادتنا في جحودِ
الأشياء.
الوقتُ لا يفزعنا.
سنخرجُ زمنِ الأجداد،
نشحذ به الأحفاد.
نحن أمةٌ
لا تتجاوز.
تبقي الأشياءُ منكسرةً.
وترهفُ السمع.
لستُ مروّضةً
على تفادي
الموت.
إنه يترك
الزمن متعفنا.
في حنجرتي
في الموت
أشمُّ عفنَ العالم
أمامَ فضاء الدم.
هل تلاشت أغنياتُك،
أم أن الوقتَ
التقطها قبل العفن!
لو شئتُ أن أهبك

letting it seep into their color.
They endure the falling of their leaves,
They do not rot.
They awaken with branches
that love their stretching.
We refuse to age,
we refuse to extend,
as usual, in our denial
of things.
Time does not scare us.
We will invoke the time of ancestors,
to excite their descendants.
We are a nation
that does not let go.
Things remain broken
and they listen carefully.
I am not trained
to avoid
death.
It leaves
time rotten.
In my throat,
in death,
I smell the rot of the world
in front of the space of blood.
Have your songs vanished,
or has time
snatched them before the rottenness?!
If I wished to gift you
a tune,
which piece would match your smile?

نغمة
أيةِ مقطوعةٍ تقارب ابتسامتك؟
تعلمتُ أدمن
ذوبانَ وجعك
وقطرات المطر
الظلُّ يتعفن
في بقايا تمدّدِه
الليلُ
من دونك مخيفٌ
في تعفّنِه.
الحبُّ ببطءٍ
أو الموتُ
كلاهما طريقٌ
مختصرٌ للعفن.
أنشغلُ بك
بماذا سأرمي
بطاقاتِ الحياة الاستفزازية؟

الرعبُ ما تركته لي.
أبحث في عزلتي
كمن راهن
على الفجيعةِ مرّةً
وكسرَ عمرَه مرات.
سكن حصارُ الحبر
مكتظّاً بشاعريةٍ
تصكُّ جلدَها
في قشرة الأرض.
تبحثُ عن ضحكاتك

I've learned to be addicted
to the melting of your pain
and raindrops.
The shadow rots
in the remains of its stretching.
The night,
without you, is terrifying
in its rottenness.
Loving slowly,
or dying,
are both shortcuts to rottenness.
I am preoccupied with you.
With what will I throw
provocative life cards?
Terror is what you've left me.
I search in my solitude
like one who bet
on tragedy once
and broke his life multiple times.
The siege of ink rests,
full of romanticism,
and strikes its skin
on the earth's crust,
searching for your laughter.

مجازات شرقية
فيوليت أبو الجلد - لبنان

المشهد الفرنسي مهذب ومشذب هذا الصباح،
أسير بلغة عربية جامحة
أعبر نحو الفكرة بخطوة مترجمة
أعود منها بخطوتين وحيرة.
التيه يجعل الشعر ممكنا
أستدلّ من المارّة على الطرقات بمجازات شرقية
أعثر عليّ في السؤال لا في الجواب،
تلتبس علينا اللغة
ونلتئم في ابتسامات متبادلة،
في موسيقى الوداع.
الحدائق الفرنسية مهذبة ومشذبة
وأنا أعشق بلغة عربية جامحة
أغرق في جحيم العبارات الخادشة للحياء الأوروبي
كلما مسّني جنّ من أحب.
أنا رهان بين إله وملاك سقط فجأة
في مونولوغي الخاص،
راح يترجم شرودي بلغات كثيرة
ورحت أضحك عاليا
أحب أعلى
وأشتم كثيرا
بلهجة وحيدة

Middle Eastern Metaphors
Violette Abou Jalad – Lebanon
   (co-tr. by Amir Al-Azraki and Jennifer Jean)

This French scene is refined and pruned, this morning—
I walk in an unruly Arabic,
cross toward notions with a translated step,
and step back twice, puzzled.

Wandering makes poetry possible:
I learn from pedestrians with Middle Eastern metaphors,
manners, gestures. I find myself in questions,
not in answers:

but, "I" and "me" are muddled by the tongue,
are converged by mutual smiles
and *bon voyage* ballads.
This French garden is refined and pruned,

this morning. I adore it in a wild Arabic.
I sink into an inferno of phrases
offensive to Europeans
whenever I'm touched by the jinn of love;

whenever I'm a wager
between a god and an angel, suddenly falling
into a private monologue,
translating my escape into many languages.

So, I start
laughing a high-pitched laugh,
and love more,
insult more

in a single dialect.

لديهم قصصهم
أسماء حسين - مصر

لديه ما يقوله لي باب الغرفة
يصدر صوتًا حين ألمسه، كما لو أنه
يحاول أن يحكي لي قصته البائسة مع الفأس
قبل أن يعرف جسده لمسات أخرى.
لديها ما تقوله لي زجاجات طلاء الأظافر:
اعدلي بيننا.. في رؤية العالم
كيف يبدو من أطراف يديكِ.
لديه ما يقوله لي النمل
الذي كلما رآني شاردة أفكر، يخاف،
لفرط وحدتي
من أن يصدر ضجة حين يجرّ حبة السمسم
التي سقطت على الأرضية:
اعذري تطفلنا عليكِ.
لديه ما يقوله لي الكتاب المفتوح
على الصفحة الثانية والسبعين منذ أيام طوال:
هناك تبديل في الأحداث، صارت أكثر تشويقًا.. عودي!
لديها ما تقوله لي الذبابة المزعجة
التي تلعق بقايا نظراتي عن الحائط:
شكرًا لمآسي العالم
التي جعلتك تشعرين بالأسى علينا
وتتمهلين قبل استعمالك للمبيد الحشري.

They Have Their Stories
Asmaa Hussain – Egypt
(co-tr. by Mohamed Hassan and Jennifer Jean)

The door has something to tell me.
The door makes a sound when I touch it, as if it is
trying to say its sob story with the ax
before its body knew touch.
The nail polish has something to tell me:
Be fair ... see the world
from your fingertips!
The ants have something to tell me.
The ants note my absent-mindedness, fear
my severe loneliness,
and the sound of a dragged sesame seed
fallen to the floor:
Forgive our intrusion.
The open book has something to tell me
days ago, on page seventy-two:
Events have twisted. They're more riveting. Come back!
The maddening flies have something to tell me.
They lick the remains of my gaze off the wall:
We are grateful for world tragedies
making you feel bad
slowing you down before you spray insecticide.

الصباح الحزين
سلوى بن رحومة - تونس

صباح الربيع الحزين
وأم تقطف من الأرض صوت الرضيع
تزايد من يشتري ثديها
والحليب
ووزير يبارك دمعتها
يهديها آخر حضن الأمومة
يضيف على جرحها
ملحا وفلفلا
أسود من ليلها المستحيل
تراود كردونة أن أفيقي
ورددي كلمة الوداع الأخير

The Sad Morning
Salwa ben Rhouma – Tunisia
   (co-tr. by Mohamed Hassan and Jennifer Jean)

A sad spring morning
and a mother retrieves from the earth the sound of her infant.
The bidding increases her heart
and milk,
and a minister blesses her tears,
gifts her the last embrace of motherhood,
adds to her wound,
salt—and pepper
blacker than her impossible night.
She pleads with the contents of the cardboard box to awaken
and utter a final farewell.

مشطي رأسي جيدًا
مروى أبو ضيف - مصر

مشطي رأسي جيدًا
مرري أصابعك بين كل خصلة
ضعي رأسي على ساقيك تحت الشمس الحارقة
حتى و إن سكبت كل هذا الجازولين في فمي
هذه ميتة جميلة
يملؤها الحنين والذكريات المبهجة
لا ليست أمي التي لم أعرفها يومًا
إنها الغولة
و عقلة الإصبع
و قبيلة هادرة من الفئران في السقف العالي
بين جذوع النخل و المواويل الكثيرة
طلقات الرصاص العائلية
و أشباح الترعة البعيدة
النداهة التي تختار رجالها بعناية مستفزة
"أم الشعور" التي لا يشفع عندها حب و لا دموع
والخبز الصعيدي الغليظ
بطعمه الجاف في الحلق
ااااه القهوة مرة جدا
لكني أحب قهوتي مرة
وأشباحي حادة ومفزعة
كل هؤلاء القراصنة المقتولين
اسكبي الجازولين على هذا الكابوس
لم أحبه يوما
بين أسنان المشط
يسقط الجاثوم
يسقط القمل والأفكار الخائبة

Comb My Hair Well
Marwa Abo daif – Egypt
(co-tr. by Mohamed Hassan and Jennifer Jean)

Comb my hair well,
run your fingers through each strand,
place my head on your lap under a scorching sun.
Even if you pour gasoline in my mouth,
this a beautiful death
filled with nostalgia and joyful memories.
No, not of my mother whom I never knew,
but the ogre,
and the Hop-o'-My-Thumb,
and a thundering tribe of rats in the high ceiling
between the palm trunks and many songs—
the family gunshots,
the ghosts on the distant canal,
the mermaid who chooses her men with maddening care,
the water nymph who spares neither love nor tears,
and the coarse Upper Egyptian bread,
with its dry taste in the throat.
Ah, the coffee is very bitter,
but I love my coffee bitter,
and my ghosts sharp and terrifying,
all these murdered pirates
pouring gasoline on this nightmare.
I never loved anything
between the teeth of a comb,
and down with the nightmare,
and down with the lice and failed thoughts.

يستيقظ الله في رأسي
نعم اشهقي هكذا
و الطمي خديك و صدري
سقط رماني من زمن مضى
في حريق الصعيد الكبير
لما صعدت الغولة من البئر
خطفت الصغار
كانت معركة هائلة
حسمتها النداهة بأغنية واحدة
آه يا حبيبي
سقطت في الترعة وراءك ولم أجدك
سقطت في البحر وراءك ولم أجدك
سقطت في البئر وراءك ولم أجدك
مشطي رأسي جيدًا
يسقط القمل والأفكار الخائفة
وضعت الحجر في جيبي
رفعني الماء للسماء
وضعت الرصاصة في فمي
هزت جسدي المواويل فرقصت
وضعت الدواء في معدتي
نما في أحشائي جنينا
صرت أمّا

God awakens in my head.
Yes! I gasped like that,
and slapped your cheeks and my chest.
A pomegranate fell from the past
from the great fire of Upper Egypt
when the ogre rose from the well,
snatched the little ones.
It was a tremendous battle,
settled by the mermaid with a single song.
Ah, my love,
I fell into the canal behind you and did not find you,
I fell into the sea behind you and did not find you,
I fell into the well behind you and did not find you.
Comb my hair well.
Comb out the lice and the fearful thoughts.
I put stones in my pockets,
water lifted me to the sky.
I put a bullet in my mouth,
and songs shook my body, I danced
and put medicine in my belly.
As a fetus grew in my bowels,
I became a mother.

أمومة افتراضية
هدى الدغفق - السعودية

سأصور أطفالي الذين
لم يأتوا بعد
بملامحي الممحوة في عدسة العائلة
حين مسها الوعاظ.
سأعرض لقطاتهم في
أشهر المواقع الالكترونية
لتربيهم التقنية
بملامح
شعب حر.

Hypothetical Motherhood
Huda Aldaghfag – Saudi Arabia
(co-tr. by Mohamed Hassan and Jennifer Jean)

I will photograph my children, who
have not arrived,
who'll filter my awful, family features
touched by preachers.
I will share their shots
on the best of the famous websites
so technology will raise them
to look like
a free people.

كما في الحرب
إيمان السباعي - مصر

هذه الشقة صحراء
تنقطع الكهرباء فتلمع عيون الذئاب
أحدهم يرفع الأغطية
ثعبانٌ طريّ يتحرك حولي
تُفتح الشرفة فتدخل فرقة بدائية بموسيقاها
وإلهٌ من لحمٍ ودم يسقط على الفراش.

الاستيقاظ في بيت غريب
تدريب جيد على التخلص من ولعك بالمرآة
فمرآة الغريب لا تعكس سوى صورة صاحبها
أنا خائفة
أحاول الاحتفاظ بصورة وجهي في الذاكرة
حتى أتعرف إليه عندما أعود إلى البيت
أما جسدي
فهو جسد الغريب
عاريًا، ونيّئًا بين أسناني.

أنا معلقة من قدميّ وتحتي بركان
أنا مقيدة اليدين ورأسي بين فخذيّ
عرقي ساخن ورائحتي حامضة
كرائحة العذاب في جوفك
"تحدثي إليّ"
تقول
وأنت تقذف كائناتك الكرنفالية في وجهي
الكلمات الملعونة
الكلمات الحارقة

As in War
Iman Alsebaiy – Egypt
   (co-tr. by Mohamed Hassan and Jennifer Jean)

This apartment is a desert.
The power goes out and the eyes of wolves gleam.
Someone lifts the covers,
a supple snake moves around me.
The balcony opens and a primitive band with its music enters,
and a god of flesh and blood falls onto the bed.

Waking up in a strange house
is good training to lose your fascination with the mirror.
For a stranger's mirror only reflects the stranger's image.
I'm scared
and try to keep the image of my face in my memory
so I can recognize it when I get home.
But my body
is the body of the stranger—
naked, raw between my teeth.

I am hanging by my feet and beneath me is a volcano,
my hands are bound and my head is between my thighs,
my sweat is hot and my scent is sour
like the smell of torment within you.
Talk to me,
you say,
as you hurl your carnivalesque beings at my face—
the cursed words,
the scorching words.

حلقي جاف ولساني مشقوق
هذا الفحيح هو الحب!

وأنت داخلي سأبكي
وأتذكر النسيان
أتذكر جنيني الميت في دمي
لم ينجذب طفلي للمرايا
كان يتجنب المرور أمامها كأنه وحده
من يمكنه رؤية شياطين مخيفة تسكنها
عندما استطاع أن يصوّب كرةً
كانت المرآة ضحيته
احتاج الأمر إلى أكثر من مرآة
حتى أعتادَ على مرايا البيت المهشمة
أتأمل صورتي الغريبةَ فيها
ألا تشبه صورةً فوتوغرافية مزقها شخصٌ غاضب
ثم أعاد تجميع أجزائها؟

أعرف أنني أخبرتك بهذا من قبل
"أنا أكره جسدي
جسد الطفلة الذي انفتح لأصابع مدرس الموسيقى
وتلصّص على محاولات الجارة استثارة الزوج الأعمى
مرةً، خلعت ملابسي ونمت مع جثة رجل في الجريدة
تخيلته يعتليني قبل أن تضرب القذيفة بيته.
لماذا لا أستطيع أن أنسى
النظرات الشبقة للتماثيل؟

هذه الشقة صحراء
وأنا أريد أن أذهب معك إلى شقة في حيّ سكنيّ
تتوسطها سجادة كثيفة تبلع أقدامنا
ويطل منها قطيع أُسود يطارد غزالة

My throat is dry and my tongue is split.
This hissing is love!

When you are inside me, I will cry
and remember forgetting,
remember the dead fetus in my blood.
My child was not drawn to mirrors,
avoided passing them as if alone
he could see the terrifying demons inhabiting them.
When he managed to aim a ball,
the mirror was his victim.
It took more than one mirror
before he got used to the shattered mirrors of the house.
I gaze at my strange image in them.
Doesn't it resemble a photograph torn by an angry someone,
then pieced back together?

I know I have told young folks,
I hate my body.
The child's body that opened to the music teacher's fingers,
and spied on the neighbor's attempts to arouse her blind husband.
Once, I stripped and slept with the corpse of a man in the newspaper,
imagined him on top of me before the shell hit his home.
Why can't I forget
the lascivious stares of statues?

This apartment is a desert.
And I want to go with you to an apartment in a suburban neighborhood
with a thick carpet in the middle that swallows our feet
and portrays a lion pack chasing a deer.

أريد أن أتعلق بظهرك وتحملني كغوريلا
وأن يمحو ضجيج الشارع لهاثي وصرخاتي كلها.
كما تحب
ستكون الجدران من زجاج
رأيت هذا في فيلم:
جسدان عاريان يلتحمان والسجناء يلوحون لهما
ويشجعونهما على الاستمرار بإشاراتٍ بذيئة.

أنا لست خائفة يا راسبوتين
أنا لست خائفة يا دو ساد
كل ما في الأمر أنني سأتقيأ!

لماذا نقول الشقة ولا نقول البيت
لأن البيت يجب أن تكون له حديقة
ويجب أن يكون به طفل يبكي في حجرته عندما يعنّفه أبوه
طفل شرير يخنق القطة البيضاء المسكينة
هذه القطة هي كل ما تبقى لي
قطعوا لسانها وما زالت تموء في الليل
وهي تشاهدني أفرغ مائي بيدي
ثم أبكي.

أحب أن تلجني حتى أنقّط دمي في البانيو
وأتركه يختلط بالماء فيصبح لونه ورديًّا
كمثل فم دجاجة
ساقاي لن تحملاني طويلاً
بعد أن انهارت فوقهما كل هذه المنازل
يرتعشان فأستند إلى السيراميك
تلسعني البرودة وأنا ألتقط صورًا لأظافري تحكُّ جلدي
عروقك نافرة يا حبيبي
هل تؤلمك

I want to cling to your back as you carry me like a gorilla,
while the street noise erases my panting and all my screams.
As you wish,
the walls will be glass.
I saw this in a movie:
two naked bodies connecting and the prisoners waving at them,
urging them—with obscene gestures—to continue.

I am not afraid, Rasputin,
I am not afraid, de Sade,
It's just that I'm going to throw up!

Why do we say apartment and not house?
Because a house should have a garden,
should have a child crying in his room when his father scolds him,
a mischievous child strangling the poor white cat.
This cat is all that is left to me
and they cut her tongue. But at night she meows
as she watches me stimulate my waters with my hands,
then cry.

I love for you to penetrate me until I bleed in the bathtub,
my blood mixing with the water, turning it pink
like the mouth of a hen.
My legs will not hold me for much longer
after all these homes collapse on them.
They tremble and I lean on the ceramic,
the cold stinging as I snap photos of my nails scratching my skin.
Your veins are bulging, sweetheart—
do they hurt,

هل تنفجر وتلطخ السقف؟
سأقضي ليلتي كلها في تنظيف البقع الزرقاء
مختنقة برائحة الديتول
وأنا أغني للحب.

تزعجني المسافة بين يدي وكأس الماء
أمد ذراعي حتى آخرها ولا أطاله
وأظل أفكر في ظمأي
وأبلل شفتيّ الجافتين بلساني
أريد أن أترك السرير وأمشي إلى أن أصل إليه
لكن التفكير يغريني بالمزيد من التفكير
والشرخ في حلقي يمنعني من مناداتك لإنقاذي
أستسلمُ
وأشعر أن مشاهدة الماء في الكأس متعة حقيقية
وأنني لو متُّ الآن سأكون سعيدة حقًّا.

لماذا لا نعيش في فندق بُني على أنقاض حيّ دُمّر في القصف؟
أو نعيش في سيارة؟
سنرفع صوت الموسيقى
ونتجاهل الموق الذي يلوّحون لنا على الطرق السريعة
أسنانهم صفراء ورائحتهم نتنة وفي عيونهم فزع
بمرور الوقت، لن نشعر بالذنب
سنتجاوز هذا كله وننام بعمق على سرير نظيف
كان لعروسين تزوجا حديثًا
سوف أستيقظ في الليل وأحدق في عيني سمكة الزينة
ثم أتأملك نائمًا
أنت الصبي الفاتن في رواية (Death in Venice)
أمد يدي بين ساقيك وأتلوى من الألم وأموت
أمد يدي بين ساقيّ وألمس هذا الدمل الصغير
كزهرة نابتة

will they burst and stain the ceiling?
I will spend the whole night cleaning the blue stains,
Choking on the scent of Dettol
as I sing to love.

The distance between my hand and the water glass bothers me.
I extend my arm to its limit and yet cannot reach it.
I keep thinking about my thirst,
and moisten my dry lips with my tongue.
I want to leave the bed and walk until I reach the water,
but thinking tempts me to think more,
and my dry throat prevents me from calling you to save me.
I give up,
and feel that watching the water in the glass is a true pleasure,
and if I died now, I would be truly happy.

Why don't we live in a hotel built on the ruins of a bombed neighborhood?
Or live in a car?
We will turn up the music
and ignore the dead waving at us on highways.
Their teeth are yellow and they stink—there is terror in their eyes.
Over time, we will not feel guilty.
We will get past this and sleep deeply on a clean bed
belonging to newlyweds.
I will wake at night and stare into the eyes of the fish in the tank,
I will watch you sleeping,
you are the beautiful boy in that *Death in Venice* novel.
I extend my hand between your legs and writhe in pain and die.
I extend my hand between my legs and touch this small pimple,
like a budding flower.

فيعتلّ وينكمش تحت جلدي
أشعر بتوتراته الواهنة داخلي
أحبس أنفاسي من الخوف وأتشبث بجسدك
جسد الطفل
جسد الصبي
جسد الرجل
جسد المرأة.
لا يوجد مكان أشد كآبة من غرفة في فندق بُني حديثًا
لا يوجد مكان أكثر رعبًا من سيارة على طريق سريع
لا مكان سوى هذا الجسد.

But it gets weaker and shrinks beneath my skin.
I feel its feeble tensions inside me,
hold my breath fearfully and cling to your body,
the body of a child,
the body of a boy, the body of a man,
the body of a woman.
There is no place gloomier than a room in a newly built hotel,
no place more terrifying than a car on a highway,
there is no place but this body.

موت قيصريّ
سوزان شكرون - لبنان

تَوارى عن أنظار ظلّه متخفيّاً وراء نسمة!
سَكَّنَ أوراق الخريف ليحمله أرَقٌّ أصفرُ إلى رصيفِ حلم ذات مساء...
تطايرت أيامه الذابلة فوق رأسه وهوَ متشبِّثٌ بعرقِ غيمة!
تعدو الخاطرات أمام نَعَسِه ويُطلِق العَنانَ للطريق... ويمشي!
يحتمي بسنبلة متأرجحة، حمقاء في شموخها، ولكنّها مشرقة!
ربّما الآمال الباقية على الدروب تنتظر من يلملمها... وربّما للمُعدَم حقُّه في مطلبٍ أخيرٍ قبل إسدال المشنقة على مسرح وجوده!
كلُّنا رزمٌ محكمة التوضيب بإذن خالقٍ أعلى.. ما إن يفتح علينا عقدة الغلاف حتّى تسبح حياتنا من أمامنا سيلاً من دمِ الأحلام!!!
من عليه أن يقطع حبل الصرّة حينها؟ سماؤنا أم الأقدار؟؟؟
لا إجابة واضحة...
الحياة عقيمة بلا مشوار...
الدرب عاقر بلا وجوهنا...
وجهه بقي
مستتراً بلا ظلّه،

Cesarean Death
Suzanne Chakaroun – Lebanon
   (co-tr. by Julia Gettle and Mahmoud Nowara)

He disappeared out of sight of his shadow, hidden behind a breeze!
He lived among the autumn leaves to be carried by a yellow insomnia to the sidewalk of an evening dream ...
His withered days flew above his head as he clung to the sweat of a cloud!
Thoughts race in front of his drowsiness as he releases the reins to the road ... and walks!
He shelters in a swinging ear of wheat, foolish in its loftiness, though it shines!
Perhaps the remaining hopes on the paths await someone to collect them ... and perhaps to the destitute goes the right of a final request before the gallows is lowered on the stage of his existence!
We are all tightly packaged by order of a higher creator ... and when the package is opened, our lives swim before us as a torrent of dream blood!!!
Who, then, should cut the umbilical cord? Our sky or our destinies???
No clear answer ...
Life is infertile without a journey ...
The path is barren without our faces ...
His face remains
Hidden without his shadow ...
Tonight my face is featureless!

ولادة
هدى عبد القادر محمود - مصر

عندما
ولدتني أمي
لم تكن
تعرف
أنها أنجبت
الخوف
توْأماً............. لي
لم تكن................. تعرف
أنه تسلسل خلسة منها
وهي تصارع آلام المخاض
ليستقر
بين أضلعي
وعندما
أرضعتني أمي
لم تكن تعلم
أنه يرتشف
الحصة الأكبر
حتى بات
خوفي أكبر مني

Birth
Hoda AbdelKader Mahmoud – Egypt
(co-tr. by Mohamed Hassan and Jennifer Jean)

When
my mother gave birth to me,
she did not
know
she gave birth to
fear,
a twin ... to me.
She did not ... know
it secretly sneaked away,
when she struggled in labor,
and settled
between my ribs.
When
my mother breastfed me,
she did not know
the fear suckled
the largest share,
until my fear
became larger than me.

كيف سنكتب عن الحب - الجزء ٤
فيوليت أبو الجلد - لبنان

جديرون بالنقوش المحفورة على أضرحتنا،
سنعود لنخدع الأحياء
بسيَر ذاتية مليئة بالأخطاء.
نحن أبناء الخوف
أطلقنا العنان للمخيّلة
وحبسنا أقدامنا بأحذية ضيقة.
سنعود لنمرّغ بالتراب أجسادنا،
لنقامر بأسرّتنا الدافئة
بمقاعدنا
بأوراقنا،
لنرهن بيوتنا للريح
أقرباءنا للغرباء.
سنعود على هيئة طيور،
على هيئة حقول ونمتد جبالًا ووديانًا.
سنعود على هيئة قلوب وننكسر
ألف مرة نلتئم ونعود ننكسر.
سنعود على هيئة رصَد
سنكون الكنز والماضي والسرّ
سنكون الأشباح التي تلهو الآن وسط هذا النص
بعد موتنا.

How to Write of Love, Part 4
Violette Abou Jalad – Lebanon
(co-tr. by Julia Gettle and Mahmoud Nowara)

Worthy of the epigraphs engraved on our shrines,
We will return to deceive the living
With resumes full of errors.
We are the children of fear
We unleashed the imagination
And locked our feet in tight shoes.
We will return to wallow our bodies in the dirt,
To gamble with our warm beds
With our seats
With our papers,
To mortgage our homes to the wind
Our relatives to strangers.
We will return in the form of birds,
In the form of fields and extend into mountains and valleys.
We will return in the form of hearts and break
A thousand times we heal and break again.
We will return in the form of observation
We will be the treasure, the past, and the secret
We will be the ghosts that play now in the middle of this text
After our death.

الموسيقار والعصفور
خولة جاسم الناهي - العراق

- لنعقد اتفاقاً يا صديقي:
أنت تعلمني الغناء
وأنا أهبك الحرية
- ما رأيك أن تكتفي بالعزف
وأنا من سيعلمك الحرية
فالسجن ليس إلا ما تضع نفسك فيه
وذو الأجنحة سيطير حتى في الأقفاص

The Musician and the Sparrow
Khawla Jasim Alnahi – Iraq
   (co-translated by Abeer Abdulkareem and Dzvinia Orlowsky)

—Let's agree, my friend:
You teach me to sing
And I'll gift you with freedom

—How about you just play?
And I'll be the one to teach you freedom
Prison is of your own making
Those with wings fly even in cages

حمد والطريق الى المجزرة
أزهار علي حسين - العراق

مهداة إلى شهداء سبايكر

تناسل الملح
لأن الأرض عطشى
والصيف خائن
الجنوبيون نحن
رتقنا الخيبات بالأحلام
والموت بالأهازيج
مازلنا نبذل للريح أبناءنا
وهي تبحث عن حطب لنيران عواصفها
تشابهت الأيام أم أنك بعد لم تكبر يا حمد؟
غصت الأرض بكذابين أكفاء
وكواكب مظللة
وأكف تلطمك بالأبواب الموصدة
وظلال تقتات على طولك
بياض الصيف ضاق
ولم يمنحك كفناً
آه من الأرض لم تحوِك يا حمد
مغمس أنت برائحة الشيلة
والنواعي
ودللول.. دللول وعدوك!!!
آه من عدوٍ أسكن جثمانك المجهول
دللول دللول حمد وبيا كاع مكتول
علقت ضفائر التمر حرزا
ولبست ثوب القصب
وخطت المواويل ليلا طويلا
دربا إلى عينيك يا حمد

Hamad on His Way to the Massacre
Azhar Ali Hussein – Iraq
 (co-tr. by Amir Al-Azraki and Jennifer Jean)

Dedicated to the martyrs of the Camp Speicher Massacre

Salt is spreading, for the earth is thirsty. The summer is a traitor—
we Southerners are mending

disappointments with dreams
and death with songs—we continue sacrificing our sons to the wind
which seeks kindling to feed its firestorm.

Haven't days gone by? Haven't you grown older, oh
Hamad? The earth is filled with

expert liars and misguiding starts, hands slamming doors in your face.
Shadows scavenge on your shadow.
The summer brightness ran out and it did not give you a shroud. Oh Hamad,

woe to the earth that does not contain you. Your body
is immersed in the smell of the Sheila
and wailing, *Dililul, Dililul* . . . Woe
to your enemy who cast aside your body
in some unknown place. *Dililul*, Hamad—
where is your murdered body?

I hang date-palm fruit like a charm. I wear the reeds of our country like a dress.
Keening has drawn a long night, a path to your eyes.
And because my lamentations are love,
your heart is bigger than a prayer,

ولأن المواويل عشق
كان صدرك أوسع من صلاة
وأعظم من معجزة
أنا الجنوبية الفارهة الانتظار
كرغيف أنضج على نيرانه
أهدهدهم في المهود وفي القبور
هززت الجذع ورفعت عيني
فلا رطب تساقط
ولا رأتني عين الإله
الملح مكيدة
وكان فخك أن قالوا عنك نشمي
فماذا سأكتب فوق قبرك يا حمد؟
ألأقول باسم الملح ضاع؟
ألأقول باسم الأرض ضاع؟
ألأقول باسم الله ضاع؟
وأين لي بقبرك يا حمد؟؟؟

greater than a miracle. I am the Southerner, a monument
to the endless wait—like a loaf baked on the waiting

fire. I lull children in cribs and graves,
shake the trunk, look upwards but no ripe date falls,

nor does the eye of God see me. The salt is treacherous, is
your trap. They described you as chivalrous—

so, what shall I write on your grave, Hamad?
Shall I say: for the salt you were lost?
Shall I say: for the country, you were lost?
Shall I say: for God, you were lost? Oh Hamad,

where will I find your grave?!

٤٥٠ قتيلا ووردة
ليلى الأهدب - السعودية

يتكثف الكلام
يتحول لغيمة
لكنها الريح تتبدد
ولا يبقى إلا السكون
مستديرا
وهادئا
ووحيدا

في الغيمة تغرق وحدك
لا يبلل مطرها ورد الذاكرة
ولا يتبدى في الكيبورد وجه القمر

يتراكم الغضب
لكنه لا يصعد الدرج
ولا يطرق الباب

فالعالم مشغول - معك - بإحصاء القتلى
ولم يفطن أحد للوردة التي ذبلت في الصندوق
هكذا تربح الحرب
٤٥٠ قتيلا ووردة

450 Dead and a Rose
Laila Alahdab – Saudi Arabia
(co-tr. by Mohamed Hassan and Jennifer Jean)

Words condense,
they become a cloud,
but the wind blows,
and only stillness remains
round,
calm,
and lonely.

In the cloud, you drown alone.
Its rain does not moisten the roses of memory,
nor does the face of the moon appear on the keyboard.

Anger accumulates,
but it does not go up the stairs,
nor does it knock on the door.

For the world is busy—with you—counting the dead.
No one notices the rose that wilted in the box.
Thus, the war wins
450 dead and a rose.

جبل من خوف
سمية الشيباني - الكويت

أخاف لو أحببتك أكثر
أتعثّر باسم نبيك المتدثر بكلمات لم تفلح بستر عورة القبيلة
أخاف أن أتمرد على اللوح
ويجوع سيفك المسلول
أخاف أن تذبل بقايا أوراقي
وتذرو الريح كلماتي
وأموت قبل أن أبلغ نشوة النبوة

أخاف لو أحببتك أكثر
أكره عيني
ولن أشتاق لصوتي
وأغلق أبواب جسدي
أخاف أن أحب فيك إهمالك
فيتراكم الغبار على جسدي
وأتحول لإله من حجر وتكسرني يدٌ طاغية
أخاف لو مت فيك
أتحول لجدار
يتوسّدني سائح عجوز لالتقاط صورة للذاكرة
أخاف لو ذهبت إليك لا أجدني
أخاف الفراق الخبيث
أخاف أن أموت من الحسرة فيك
أخاف أن أموت وأنت لا تكترث

لا تأتِ
تشرب نخب غيري
وعندي تموت لغتك

A Mountain of Fear
Sumia al Shaybani – Kuwait
    (co-tr. by Amir Al-Azraki and Jennifer Jean)

I'm afraid if I love you more
I'll stumble on the name of the prophet
who is covered with words
that fail to hide the nakedness of the tribe.

I'm afraid to rebel against the Tablet,
to let your sword starve, let my leaves wither,
let the wind whip my words
before I reach the climax of prophecy.

I'm afraid if I love you more
I'll hate my eyes
then close the doors of my body
without missing my voice.

I'm afraid to love the negligence in you,
to let that dust cover my body—
turn me into a god of
stone to be smashed by a tyrant.

I'm afraid I will die in you
and turn into a wall
against which an old tourist rests
to take pictures for his memories.

I fear that if I go to you, I will not

أخاف أن أكبر وأذبل كوردة في إناء الانتظار
أخاف أن يأتي المساء وتمطر السماء وأنت لست معي
وتضيق على حزني الأرصفة
أخاف اللعنة
حتى اللعنة معك لها طعم طين أهلي
أخاف لو مر الوقت وأنا أرتل صلواتك أنسى جسدي في معبدك
وأنت تمر على عجل ولا تراني
أخاف أن يزحف ظلي إليك
وأبقى وحيدة
أخاف أن يتمرد قلبي ويرتب حقيبة سفر صغيرة ويرحل إليك
أخاف أن يأتي يوم
تصير أنت النبي
ويطردني الله من جنته
وتصبح وحدك مالك الشجرة

find myself. I fear separation. I fear
dying of the sorrow
in you—I fear death by indifference.

Don't come! Don't toast me!
Your words are dead.
Your language makes me
afraid of wilting in the vase of waiting.

I'm afraid of evening, of rain approaching
without you. Sidewalks narrow at my sorrow.
Your curse tastes as sweet as my family mud.
I fear time passing as I say your prayers.

I forget my body in your temple
as you hurry past, unseeing
me. I fear my shadow creeping to you,
leaving me alone.

I fear my heart will rebel, take a travel bag,
go to you. I'm afraid of you
becoming the prophet. And God
expelling me from His paradise

because you alone own the tree of life.

فأر تجارب
منى العاصي - فلسطين

تسألني الحرب: كيف أنت يا منى
لا جديد أيتها الحرب
ها أنا في قفص التجارب
أربي في مخيلتي
غرفتين وصالة
شرفة لحبق أمي
وعائلة صغيرة
أراكم الأنهار
لأغسل القميص الأخير لأخي
وأكدس علب المورفين
لِتُصْلِحَ رِفًّا
في خاصرة أختي
أرتب أقدام طفلتي
في كرسيها الواقف في حلقي
ولن أنسى
أن أبي له من السيقان
ما يكفي لئلا
أتعثّر

Guinea Pig
Muna Alaasi – Palestine
   (co-tr. by Dima AlBasha and Jennifer Jean)

The war asks, *How are you, oh Muna?*
Oh war... Nothing new
here. I'm in the trial's cage,
reviving my memory
of two bedrooms & a salon,
& a balcony for my mom's basil
& a small family.
I use up the rivers
to wash the last of my brother's shirts.
& I pile the morphine boxes
that fix the ridge in my sister's pelvis.
I keep my girl's feet
in her wheelchair—which stands in my throat.
& I won't forget
how my father had legs enough
for me not to trip.

دائرة وقت
سلمى حربة - العراق

دهشةٌ تعلو حينَ يُرتَجِلُ الزمنُ
فلا يغريني قربكَ ولا يهزني بعدكَ
أتمسك بنفحاتٍ ذابتْ في مخيلتي
استباحت صحرائي وروداً
واحاتٌ مرسومةٌ بخطوطٍ منحنيةٍ
أفقٌ خُرافي لا ينتمي لحزنِ الأرضِ
دهشةٌ تعتريهِ، لا هواء يغرقه ولا سماء تسبّح له
فراغٌ يتحدى كينونة الموت والحياة
الوقت .... آفة هذه الأرض
ماردٌ يبتلعُ كل ما حوله
لا يكترث
لا يمل
لا يتوقف
يودعُ ماشيا متسارعا منهمرا يكتسح الركود
وقفت بين طغيان مجراه أتمسك بنزر ثانية
وددت أن أسأله
أين ستتوقف؟؟ متى تلتقي بنهايتك
متى تنهي دائرة الوقت
دهشتي لم يكترث لها
كان سينهي دائرته
ويعود
ولم يعد أبداً!

The Circle of Time
Salma Abdul Hussein al-Harba – Iraq
  (co-tr. by Amira Al-Azraki and Jennifer Jean)

Astonishment emerges
when time is improvised. Love,
your closeness doesn't tempt me,
your distance doesn't shock me.
I hold tight to traces
seared into my imagination: You
invade my desert with flowers—oh,
oasis drawn in curved lines—oh,
mythical horizon, who rejects
the sadness of Earth.
You are afflicted with astonishment.
The air does not drown you,
nor does Heaven celebrate you. But, a void
can challenge life and death. And
time, who infests this earth—
is a giant swallowing everything.
He does not care.
He does not get bored.
He does not stop
walking rapidly
out to sweep away all stillness.
I stopped the tyranny
of his journey—
held onto less than a second
asked him:
Where will you stop?
When will you meet your end?
Where will the circle end?

He didn't care about my astonishment.
He was about to finish his circle and
come back.
He never came back!

في الروح أسئلةٌ مُجنّحةٌ
إيمان مصاروة - فلسطين

مابينَ صبركَ والحياةِ قصيدة
وَشْمُ السياطِ المُنتشي
دَمْعٌ يزيلُ ضبابَ مَنْ تَركوا الحِمى
يومَ الثباتْ
الروحُ تهجرُني قليلاً
في انكساراتي
وتعودُ لي بعدَ القليلِ
بما تمَالَكَ راحِلٌ
مِنْ صفعةٍ
كادَتْ بأن تُفني بردَّتِها يَمينَ الجِلد
في أكفانِ حُلم
عابرٍ لا يرِقُّ
سوى ليمضيَ شامخاً
بئسَ الحياةُ
إذا تملّكَها من الذلِّ الرعاةُ

In Souls, There Are Questions with Wings
Eman Masrweh – Palestine
 (co-tr. by Dima AlBasha and Jennifer Jean)

Between your patience & a true life, there is: an epic,

the tattoo of a satisfied whip,

tears that clear the fog of nomads who left home
on the day of solidity.
My soul abandons me a bit
when I am shards—
it comes back to me a bit after
with an awakening slap
that almost takes off the right cheek.

In the coffins of a passing dream
that doesn't soften
except to stand, long & proud—

damn the life
under a sheep herder's rule! How humiliated it is!

نبيذ المعبد
سمية الشيباني - الكويت

ساقية الحانة تسكب خمر المعبد... وتقسم بالعنب المقدس
أنني جنية بثوب امرأة
تمسح قطرات الخمر المذبوحة بمنديل أحمر وتصلي
تنظر لعيني... تلتقط كفي!
لا ترتابي... هاتي كفك..
حرائق غابات الأرز مسحت خط العودة...
هاتي كفك أقول!
مزروعة بذاكرة الطين
ثمة حزن أسود قابع بعينيك
وهذا الخط الضامر ليس سوى ندبة
كفك هذا ينبئ ببركان
لكن...
اشربي هذا الكأس
أسوار أوروك تغني
قولي لأنكيدو... أن يختصر الحكاية
ويموت بطلا
ساقية الحانة ماكرة
كساحرة تكشف أوراقي .
هذا وجه...
وهذي أنت
ألف امرأة
معتقة مثل خطوط يدي
ومثل نبيذ المعبد
ومثل نخلة بيتنا

Wine from the Temple of Ishtar
Sumia al Shaybani – Kuwait
    (co-tr. by Amir Al-Azraki and Jennifer Jean)

Shamhat pours the temple wine,
swears she's a *jinniyah*

in a gown. She wipes the slaughtered,
holy grapes with reddened tissue.

Prays, and gazes at my eyes. "Don't
be nervous," she says, "Let me

read your hands! Let me tell you
about Cedar Forest fires of no return,

that: planted in the memory of the mud,
is an endless, shadow sadness

in your eyes. This line is a scar.
Your hands speak of a volcano.

You should drink more wine.
Uruk walls are singing. You should

tell Enkidu to make the story short—
die heroically." Shamhat is sly

like a witch, revealing my secrets.
And, her face is your face,

تهاوى كل شيء من حولها
ولم تزل شاهقة
مثلي
ساقية الحانة ماكرة..

is a thousand women ripened
like the lines of my hands,

like the wine of the temple,
like the palm tree in our home.

When everything around her is falling,
she is dignified and useful

like me. Shamhat is sly.

الخياطون المهرة
فيوليت أبو الجلد - لبنان

الخياطون المهرة يلمسون أرداف النساء
برجفة خفيفة وعيون مطفأة،
يقيسون الزمن الممتدّ من اليسار الى اليمين
ببوصلة حائرة.
مَن يأخذ قياس الحزن
على صدر امرأة عامر بالسياج؟
فوق الركبتين،
تحت الركبتين،
أو حتى الكاحلين،
ما أدراك، والقماش لا يراهن على العينين
بل على تواطؤ الساقين مع الساقية
بإبرة وخيط أحمر
أرتق كل ليلة أفكار المتآمرين على بلادك،
في يدي الحقائق والأسرار والمغفرة.
أنقر على أبواب الله السحرية،
أترك على عتباتها دعائي
وأجرة الخياطين المهرة

The Skilled Tailor
Violette Abou Jalad - Lebanon
 (co-tr. by Amir Al-Azraki and Jennifer Jean)

A tailor touches a woman's hips
with a light shiver and dull eyes,
measures time from left to right

with a confused ruler.
But, who will measure the grief
in a woman's caged chest?

Above the knees...
Under the knees...
Around the ankles...

Clothing doesn't bet on the eyes
but on a conspiracy of luscious legs.
With a needle and red thread,

every night, I darn the thoughts
of conspirators
against every woman's country.

In my hands are facts,
secrets, forgivenesses.
I knock on the magical doors of God—

leave my prayers on the threshold.
Leave fees
for that Skilled Tailor.

على سفر
فاطمة بنيس - المغرب

بخطى موجعة حدّ اللذة
نسافر
نعاندُ الطريق
التي لن توصلنا
نرسمُ محطات
تذيب المسافة
ولأنّنا صمّ لبؤس العالم
لا نلتفت لمّنبّه الوصول.
ننسجُ بيتا من ريشنا
نؤثثه بأغصان حب مرتعش
نذيع بين أركانه أنين الروح.
بأصابعنا الخائفة
من فضيلة الريح
نغرس في تربته زهورا
نسقيها برضابنا.
لدينا ما يكفي من العطش
لنتقنَ فنّ الرواء
لدينا ما يكفي من النور
لنحترف العتمة
لدينا ما يكفي من الأحلام
من الأنفاس
من الأشعار
لنبقى على سفر
متدفقين كنهرين
مجرّدين من نبعهما.
اللاّيوصف ركضنا

On the Go
Fatima Bennis – Morocco
   (co-tr. by Amir Al-Azraki and Jennifer Jean)

At a painfully pleasurable pace,
we travel and challenge

the road that won't lead us.
We mark out rest stops

to resolve the distance.
And, because we're deaf to the misery

of the world, we don't pay attention
to the alarm of arrival.

We weave a house of our scant
feathers, our belongings—

furnish it with twinkling branches
of love. Within its walls,

we broadcast the soul's whimper.
With our fingers frightened

of the virtue of the wind,
we plant flowers in its loam,

water them with our spittle:
we have enough thirst

نحو تيهنا
يانعة طقوسه
آهلة بالمسرات
لبذخه
لشهده
لعصفه
خلقنا.
ها صرنا وطنا بحجم قلب
نرفع فيه راية العشق
بحمده نسبّح
ونشهد أنّ لا وطن لنا غيره

to master the art of irrigation;
we have enough light

to practice darkness;
we have enough dreams, breaths,

poems—to travel, to flow
like streams without a spring.

Running toward our lostness,
full of mellow rituals, of delights—

for this structure's loving,
lavishness, honey, blasts—

we were created. We have become
a heart-sized homeland.

We raise the standard of love—*praise
be to Him*. We

testify that there is no other
territory. And, this house is ours.

ظل
نرمين المفتي - العراق

أركض
أختبئُ في ظلّي،
و إن اكتشفوا فعلي،
هل
سيصادرون ظلّي؟
أتركه في البيت
ظلّي
أختبئُ في عيني،
يوما
اكتشفوا أنني أحلم
هددوني بقلع عيني
هل سيقلعون عيني
و هم يكتشفونني بهما
و يعتقدونني حلما؟!

A Shadow
Nermeen Al Mufti – Iraq
(co-tr. by Amira Al-Azraki and Jennifer Jean)

To run is to hide
behind my shadow.

If they discover my act,
will they seize my shadow?

Somedays, I leave it at home:
Oh, my shadow!

Hide in my eyes!
But today, they

discover I am dreaming.
They threaten

to gouge out my eyes . . .
Would they do that?

They'd discover me in my eyes.
Or they would think

I am a dream.

كيف سنكتب عن الحب - الجزء ٥
فيوليت أبو الجلد - لبنان

مجرّدُ أبوابٍ سحريّة لا تُفتح للأحبّةِ،
ولا تُغلق عليهم.
في مرفأ الغرباء ترسو المراكب
التي جذّفتْ طويلًا في الرضا.
مجرّدُ حمّى تتفشّى في الأجساد المعتمة.
حبالٌ سرّيّةٌ بين ما قلنا وما فعلنا.
مجرّدُ وقاحةٍ هذا الإسرافُ في الحبّ:
سيلٌ من الشتائم لا تترجَم إلى لغةٍ عالقةٍ في حلق الحروب،
في نشرات الأخبار،
وفي الصحفِ الساقطةِ سهوًا
من أصابع المدنِ الجميلة.
من الشبح ونقيضه يُولد الشعرُ؛
من مراكبَ جذّفتْ طويلًا في حيرةِ مَن غادروا وما غادروا؛
ومن مجرّد أبوابٍ سرّيّةٍ بين ما قلنا وما فعلنا.

How to Write of Love, Part 5
Violette Abou Jalad – Lebanon
   (co-tr. by Julia Gettle and Mahmoud Nowara)

Nothing but magic doors do not open for loved ones,
And do not close on them.
In the port of strangers the boats anchored
That had long rowed in satisfaction.
Nothing but a fever spreading through the dark bodies.
Umbilical cords between what we said and what we did.
Nothing but the audacity of this extravagance of love:
A torrent of insults that do not translate into a language stuck in the throats of wars,
In the news programs,
And in newspapers inadvertently dropped
From the fingers of beautiful cities.
From the ghost and its antithesis poetry is born;
From boats that long rowed in bewilderment of who left and what left;
And of nothing but secret doors between what we said and what we did.

أنامُ في مِحبرتي وألوّحُ للبعيد
زكية المرموق - المغرب

الذين يدخلون النارَ
بقوارب ماءٍ
الذين يلمسون السحابَ
بطائراتٍ ورقية
الذين يحشون ثقوبَ السقفِ
بالغيم
ويختبئون تحت الأسرّةِ
كلّما تلعثم في حلقِ الخطى
الطريقُ
الذين يدخلون الضبابَ
ولا يعودون من نقطة التفتيشِ
إلا بجثثِهم
الذين ينامون في محبرةٍ
كلّما ضاقَ الكلامُ
الذين كلّما تهدّلَ الجدارُ
غرسوا مساميرَ في دمِهم..
مساميرَ أكثر
كي لا تتلاشى في زحام الصمتِ
صورُ الحبيبِ
الذين يحتطبون رمادَهم
كلّما الوسادةُ تيبستْ
في الغيابِ
الذين ما تعبوا من التلويحِ
للبعيدِ...
والخرائطُ مقفلة
الذين يراودونَ العشبَ

I Sleep in My Inkwell and Wave to the Distant
Zakia el-Marmouke – Morocco
 (co-tr. by Amir Al-Azraki and Jennifer Jean)

To those who enter the fire with boats,
who touch heaven with kites,
who stuff roof holes with clouds,

who hide under beds
whenever the road stutters
in the throat of footfalls entering fog—

of footfalls that never return
from the checkpoint
which only sends back bodies;

to those who resort to the inkwell
when speech narrows,
who plant nails in their blood

whenever the wall slouches—
more and more nails
so the lover's image does not fade

into the traffic of silence;
to those who collect their own ashes
whenever their pillow is dry

whenever there's absence,
who aren't tired of waving
to loves in the distance

قبل أنْ يتغضنَ الماءُ
الذين يحتفظون بالمفاتيحِ
وهم يعرفون..
أن الأبوابَ قد سُرقتْ
الذين يتركون عكازهم
على عتبةِ الغيبِ
كلّما ودعتهم الحياة
الذين يستدلون عليهم
بالجرحِ
كلّما نامتِ الحربُ
في عيونِهم
وهي مطمئنة على رعاياها
أقول:
الغابةُ أولُها شجرة
فاترك يسراكَ نكاية بالكراسي
تصافحُ يمناكَ
ربما تُفقسُ بينهما
الأحلامُ!

whenever maps are locked;
to those who venture into meadows
before the waters flow,

who keep the keys
whenever they know the doors
were stolen, who leave their crutch

on the threshold of the unknown
whenever life leaves them behind;
to those who know themselves

through their wounds
whenever the war sleeps
in their eyes

while reassuring the subjects of war;
to all those, I say: the forest begins
with a tree; let

your left hand—which keeps the throne—
shake your right hand. Maybe
dreams hatch between them.

Acknowledgments

Consequence Forum – "Other Paths for Shahrazad" and "Hamad on His Way to the Massacre" by Azhar Ali Hussein (co-tr. by Amir Al-Azraki and Jennifer Jean); "Guinea Pig" by Muna Alaasi (co-tr. by Dima AlBasha and Jennifer Jean).

The Common – "Definitions" by Nadia Al-Katib (co-tr. by Amir Al-Azraki and Jennifer Jean); "A Pearl" and "A Shadow" by Nermeen Al Mufti (co-tr. by Amir Al-Azraki and Jennifer Jean).

Great River Review – "Mirage" by Muna Alaasi (co-tr. by Dima AlBasha and Jennifer Jean).

Poetry magazine – "I Sleep in My Inkwell and Wave to the Distant" by Zakia el-Marmouke (co-tr. by Amir Al-Azraki and Jennifer Jean).

Rattle magazine – "My Body Is Mine" by Amira Salameh (co-tr. by Yafa Al-Shayeb and Jennifer Jean).

Talking Writing magazine – "Roads Not Changed by the Feet of Walkers" by Zizi Shosha (co-tr. by Yafa al-Shayeb and Jennifer Jean); "The Jasmine Harvest" by Salma Abdul Hussein al-Harba (co-tr. by Amir al-Azraki and Jennifer Jean).

Many thanks for support and funding go to: the Her Story Is collective and Fort Point Theatre Channel—with special thanks to Amy Merrill and Marc Miller; the Massachusetts Humanities Grant organization; the Essex County Community Foundation's Creative County Initiative; Jessy Belt Saem Eldahr and the Iraqi and American Reconciliation Project; as well the Center for Arabic Culture in Boston.

The cover art was produced by Her Story Is member and Iraqi artist Thaira Al Mayahy—thank you!

Editorial Biographies

EDITOR/CO-TRANSLATOR

Jennifer Jean co-wrote and co-translated the collaborative, bilingual collection *Where Do You Live?* أين تعيش؟ with Iraqi poet Dr. Hanaa Ahmed Jabr. Other poetry collections include *VOZ*, *Object Lesson*, and *The Fool*. Her resource book is *Object Lesson: A Guide to Writing Poetry*. Her poetry, prose, and co-translations appear in *Poetry*, *Rattle* magazine, *The Common*, the *Los Angeles Review*, *Consequence Forum*, *Terrain*, and *On the Seawall*. She's received honors, residencies, and fellowships from the Kenyon Review Writers Workshop, the Academy of American Poets, the Mass Cultural Council, DISQUIET, and the Women's Federation for World Peace. Jennifer is an organizer for the artist collective Her Story Is, a faculty member at Solstice MFA, and the senior program manager of 24PearlStreet, the Fine Arts Work Center's online writing program.

MANAGING EDITOR/CO-TRANSLATOR

ABEER ABDULKAREEM is a translator, researcher, foreign language instructor, and linguist. Prior to joining Her Story Is, Abeer worked as a senior language researcher at Language Research Center in Hyattsville, Maryland, where she wrote several books on Arabic language and its dialects. Prior to this role, she taught Arabic language at Dartmouth College. She holds an MA from the Fletcher School of Law and Diplomacy at Tufts University. She was the recipient of a Fulbright Scholarship. She speaks Arabic (MSA, Iraqi, Levantine, and Egyptian).

ASSOCIATE EDITORS/CO-TRANSLATORS

AMIR AL-AZRAKI is a playwright, literary translator, Theatre of the Oppressed practitioner, and associate professor and coordinator of the Studies in Islamic and Arab Cultures Program at Renison University College, University of Waterloo. Among his plays are: *Waiting for Gilgamesh: Scenes from Iraq*, *The*

Mug, and *The Widow*. Al-Azraki is the translator of *Africanism: Blacks in the Medieval Arab Imaginary*, author of *The Discourse of War in Contemporary Theatre* (in Arabic), co-editor and co-translator of *Contemporary Plays from Iraq* and *"A Rehearsal for Revolution": An Approach to Theatre of the Oppressed* (in Arabic), and co-editor and co-translator of Arabic poetry in the *Consequence*, *The Common*, *Poetry*, and *Talking Writing*.

JULIA GETTLE is a PhD candidate in history at Brown University and a Global Islamic Studies Teaching Fellow at Connecticut College. Her dissertation charts a bottom-up history of the post-1948 Palestinian National Movement and the rise and fall of political Arab nationalism through a series of activist social biographies. Her broader scholarship focuses on Middle Eastern political and social movements, authoritarianism and security states, incarceration, displacement, and oral history.

MOHAMED ELSAWI HASSAN is a senior lecturer at the Department of Asian Languages and Civilizations at Amherst College. He received his PhD in applied linguistics from Ain Shams University, Egypt, in 2008. His research interests focus on systemic functional linguistics, critical discourse analysis, and discourse theory. He is a contributing editor of *Metamorphoses*, the journal of the Five College Faculty Seminar on Literary Translation. Recent translations include articles for *Wasla* magazine in Egypt and co-translating *African Folklore: An Encyclopedia* into Arabic.

MAHMOUD NOWARA is a freelance journalist with over 20 years' experience writing analyses, reports, and investigative pieces in Arabic and English. He is an ulti-genre, bilingual literary artist with multiple published short stories and poems and a monodrama performed in English and Arabic. He is an expert analyst of Middle East affairs who has been repeatedly consulted by print, TV, and digital media outlets. As well, he is an accomplished oral interpreter of Arabic poetry and an experienced community organizer.

POETRY CURATORS

HANAA AHMED Jabr was born in Mosul, Iraq. She is a prize-winning poet and short-story writer who has participated in critical conferences and international poetry festivals. She has a PhD in philosophy in Arabic literature. Her books include the poetry collections *My Sorrow's Reward from His Collar* and *Zahr* (*Flowers*), as well as two books of criticism: *The Dialectic of Poetry and Prose in Modernist Poetry*, and *The Poetics of the Prose Poem*. Additionally, she's released a children's book, *Sultan and Shanidar*. Hanaa teaches at the University of Mosul.

ELHAM NASSER AL-ZABEDY is a poet, visual artist, and women's rights advocate. Born in Baghdad, she graduated from the Institute of Fine Arts, Music Department, in Basra. Al-Zabedy is a leading figure in cultural activism, founding and running the Lotus Cultural Women's League. She serves as a member of the international project Her Story Is with artist Amy Miller. Her literary contributions encompass the poetry collections *Whispers of the Walnut Tree* (2008) and *Shores of the Sparrows* (2012).

RASHA FAHDIL is an award-winning short-story writer, poet, novelist, playwright, and journalist. She is currently a PhD candidate at the University of Brighton, UK, and her research focuses on the intersection of digital culture and gender identities in posthuman theatre. She was born in Basra, Iraq, in 1975 and spent her childhood there, attended college and lived for a time in Tikrit, Iraq. She holds a BA in English from the University of Tikrit and was awarded a certificate in International Journalism and Media Studies from the Institute of Arab Strategy in Beirut in 2008. Five of her books, consisting of collections of short stories, poetry, and criticism, have been published in Cairo and Syria. She is a member of the Federation of Writers in Iraq, the advisory board of the Palace of Culture and Arts in Salah al-Din (Iraq), and the International PEN Club in Berlin. She has worked for the Red Crescent and the Red Cross in Iraq at the Department of Prisoners and Detainees as well as in health education addressing AIDS prevention.

JACKLEEN HANNA (pen name Jackleen Salam) is originally from Syria and currently lives in Canada. She studied electrical engineering at Aleppo University. Her poetry collection *One Body and a Thousand Edge* was nominated for the most prestigious Arabic literature prize in the Middle East and diaspora, the Al Sheikh Zayed Prize, in 2016. Publications include *Conversations on the Mirrors of Migration*, an electronic collection of articles and 30 interviews with Canadian and Arab writers including John Ralston Saul, Rawi Hag, Walid Al Khashab, and others, published by *Winged Frog* in 2023; *One Body and a Thousand Edge*, published by Hamaleel, United Arab Emirates, in 2016; *The Inkwell Is a Female*, published by Alnahda Alarabia in 2009; *Suspicious Dancing*, published by Arabia lil Uloom in 2005, reprinted in 2022 as *She Nurtures the Clouds with Oranges*; *Crystal*, published by Al Kunooz Aladabia in 2001; and *The Fall is Shedding Mulberry Leaves*, electronically published by Almarava Althaafia in 2001. She is a member of the Writers in Exile Group and is a member of the Writer's Union of Canada and PEN Canada.

ARABIC TEXT EDITOR

MILED FAIZA is a Tunisian American poet and translator. His poetry collections include *Baqāya al-bayt alladī dakalnāhu marratan wāḥida* (2004) and *Asabaʕu an-naḥḥāt* (2019). He has translated several works by Ali Smith, including the Booker Prize-shortlisted novel *Autumn* (al-Kharif, 2017), as well as *Winter* (al-Shitā', 2019) and *Spring* (ar-Rabiʕ, 2023). He has also collaborated with Karen McNeil on translations of Amira Ghenim's *A Calamity of Noble Houses* (2025) and Shukri Mabkhout's *The Italian* (2021). Miled's poetry and translations have appeared in various Arabic and international journals, such as *WLT*, *New England Review*, *Banipal*, *Alquds al-Arabi*, and *Revue Siecle 21*. He resides in Barrington, RI, and teaches Arabic at Brown University.

CONTRIBUTING CO-TRANSLATORS

DIMA ALBASHA is an entrepreneur and translator from Aleppo, Syria. Since coming to the United States, she has become a promoter of interfaith dialogue and intercultural understanding; as well, she's given a TEDx talk that bridges gaps between people of different cultures and perspectives.

YAFA AL-SHAYEB lives in Jordan, where she is earned her BS in pharmacy. She is a volunteer for the Women's Federation for World Peace and a 2022 Lazord's Fellow for Generations for Peace (GFP), where she works as a programmes assistant. As well, she's worked with local civil associations specializing in the fields of child protection and raising awareness about gender issues. Yafa is a portrait artist and a student of the violin. In the future she plans to use the arts as a therapy when working with children who have suffered traumas.

FRANCESCA BELL is the author of *Bright Stain*, finalist for the Washington State Book Award and the Julie Suk Award, and *What Small Sound*, finalist for the Julie Suk Award and recipient of an honorable mention for the Eric Hoffer Award, and the translator of Max Sessner's *Whoever Drowned Here*, finalist for the Northern California Book Award, all from Red Hen Press. Her work appears in *ELLE*, *Los Angeles Review of Books*, and *Rattle*. She is the poet laureate of Marin County and a translation editor at the *Los Angeles Review*.

MARTHA COLLINS'S eleventh book of poetry is *Casualty Reports* (Pittsburgh, 2022); her tenth, *Because What Else Could I Do* (Pittsburgh, 2019), won the William Carlos Williams Award. Her fifth volume of co-translated Vietnamese poetry is *Dreaming the Mountain* by Tuệ Sỹ (Milkweed, 2023).

DZIVINIA ORLOWSKY is a Pushcart Prize poet, translator, and a founding editor of Four Way Books. Her sixth poetry collection, *Bad Harvest*, was a 2019 Massachusetts Book Awards "Must Read" in Poetry. She is recipient of a Massachusetts Cultural Council Poetry Grant, a Sheila Motton Book Award, and her first poetry collection, *A Handful of Bees*, was reprinted for the Carnegie Mellon University Press Classic Contemporary Series. Ali Kinsella's and her co-translations from the Ukrainian of Natalka Bilotserkivets's *Eccentric Days of Hope and Sorrow* was a 2022 Griffin International Poetry Prize finalist and their co-translations of *Lost in Living* by Halyna Kruk was awarded a 2024 NEA Literature Translation Fellowship. Dzvinia's newest poetry book, *Those Absences Now Closest*, was published by Carnegie Mellon in 2024.

DANIELLE PIERATTI is the author most recently of the poetry collection *Approximate Body* (Carnegie Mellon University Press, 2023). Her first book, *Fugitives* (Lost Horse Press 2016), was selected by Kim Addonizio for the Idaho Prize and won the Connecticut Book Award for poetry. *Transparencies*, her translated volume of works by Italian poet Maria Borio, was released by World Poetry Books in 2022. Danielle's work has been supported by the Connecticut Office of the Arts, the Bread Loaf Translators' Conference, and the Humanities Institute at the University of Connecticut. She currently serves as the poetry editor of the international literary journal, *Asymptote*.

SUSAN RICH'S most recent books include *Blue Atlas* (Red Hen Press) and *Gallery of Postcards and Maps: New and Selected Poems* (Salmon Poetry). She has co-edited *Demystifying the Manuscript: Creating a Book of Poems* (Two Sylvias Press) and *Strangest of Theatres: Poets Crossing Borders* (Poetry Foundation). Susan's previous poetry books include *Cloud Pharmacy*, *The Alchemist's Kitchen*, *Cures Include Travel*, and *The Cartographer's Tongue–Poems of the World*, winner of the PEN USA Award. A recipient of the Times Literary Supplement Award and a Fulbright Fellowship, Rich's poems appear in *New England Review*, *Ploughshares*, *World Literature Today*, and elsewhere.

CINDY VEACH is the author of *Her Kind* (CavanKerry Press), an Eric Hoffer Montaigne Medal finalist, *Gloved Against Blood* (CavanKerry Press), a finalist for the Paterson Poetry Prize and a Massachusetts Center for the Book "Must Read," and the chapbook *Innocents* (Nixes Mate). Her poems have appeared in the Academy of American Poets Poem-a-Day Series, *AGNI*, *Michigan Quarterly Review*, *Poet Lore*, *North American Review*, *Salamander*, and elsewhere. A recipient of the Philip Booth Poetry Prize and the Samuel Allen Washington Prize, she is poetry co-editor of *MER*.

Poet Biographies

ALAASI, MUNA is from Palestine. She studied English literature at Damascus University. Collections of her poems were selected as part of a global anthology published in the French and Bulgarian languages. Her translated work has been published in *Consequence Forum*. Her forthcoming poetry manuscript is *How to Raise a Window*. She is currently working on a nonfiction book about a deathly trip from Syria to Europe.

ALAHDAB, LAILA is from Saudi Arabia. Her writings include *albaHith ann yawm saabi'* (*In Search for a Seventh Day*), published by Madbouly Bookshop in 1997, *ayuun althaalib* (*Fox Eyes*), published by Dar alrayyis in 2009, *fataat an-naS* (*A Script Girl*), published by Dar Jadaaawil in 2011, *jannaat Saghira* (*Small Paradises*), published by Dar Athar in 2015, *qamiS aswad shaffaaf* (*A Black Sheer Shirt*), published by Dar Milad in 2019, and *uud Azraq* (*Blue Match*), published by Dar Rawaash in 2019. Her writings that were translated into English include *Beyond the Dunes* and *On the Weave of the Sun*, published by Strategic Book Publishing and Rights in Houston, TX.

ABO DAIF, MARWA is from Egypt. She received her BA in medicine from Ain Shams University. Her works include *thaakirat rahiil* (*Memory of Departure*), published by Dar Iktub in 2008, *iquS ayyaami wa-nthuruha fii alhawaa'* (*I Tear Out My Days and Scatter Them in the Air*), published by Dar Sharqiyat in 2013, and a joint collection with Sara Abedin, *baynana hadiqa* (*Between Us a Garden*), published by Dar Rawafid in 2016. She also contributed, with a number of Egyptian writers, to the book *alumooma* (*Motherhood*) edited by Rana al-Tunisi, published by Mirret. Some of her poems were translated into English in a book by Shirin Abo al-Naja, *Women in Revolutionary Egypt*, published by American University in Cairo.

ABD SHAFY, OMAIMA is from Egypt. She received her BA in Arabic and Islamic Studies from Al-Azhar University. Her writings include the joint collection *faqat sawiyyan* (*Only Together*) in 1999, the story collection *ba'ad maa ya'rifahu aj-jamii'* (*Some of What Everyone Knows*) in 2009, and the poetry collection *diwan alumuuma* (*Motherhood*), published by Dar Miret in 2017. She is currently the executive director of the *Gudran* Foundation for Arts and Development.

ABU JALAD, VIOLETTE is from Lebanon. Her works include *Sleep Hunter* in 2004, *The Last Violet* in 2006, *Time of the Text ... Time for the Body*, published by Fadhaa'aat Printing House in Amman, Jordan, in 2012, *I Accompany the Nuts to Their Minds*, also published by Fadhaa'aat Printing House, in 2015, *No One Lives on This Planet Except Me*, published by Alka Printing House in 2017 and soon to be published in French by Lanskin Printing House, and *Suspicions*, published by Ahliyya Printing House, Amman, Jordan. She has participated in cultural forums in Amman, Baghdad, Tunisia, Algeria, Paris, and Honduras.

ALDAGHFAG, HUDA is from Saudi Arabia. She is a literary editor and Arabic language instructor. Aldaghfag participated in several Arab and world festivals representing Saudi poetry. She is a human rights activist who frequently writes about women's rights. Her publications include *Shadow from Above* (second edition, Dar Al Mufradat, Saudi Arabia, 2002); *New Yearning* (second edition, Dar Al Mufradat, Saudi Arabia, 2002); *I Woke Up for Destiny* (Dar Alfa, Spain, 2006), which was translated into English and Spanish; *A Non-Existing Woman* (Dar Al Farabi, Beirut, 2008), which was translated into French; *A Feather that Doesn't Fly* (Dar Al Farabi, Beirut, 2008), which was translated into English; *My Face's Lake* (Dar Al Farabi, Beirut, 2008), which was translated into Spanish; *Without My Flying Pain* (Dar Ninevah, 2012); *I Tear Burqa and See* (Dar Jadawil, 2012); *Future's Philosophy* (Dar Tawa, 2014); *Hysteria of a Hypothesis* (Dar Al Ain, 2014); *I Teach My Shadow to Rebel* (Dar El Farasha, 2017); *Flying Senses* (Dar Azmina, 2017); and *I Spread My Heart on a Clothes Line* (Dar Rawashin, 2019).

AHMED JABR, HANAA was born in Mosul, Iraq. She is a prize-winning poet and short-story writer who has participated in critical conferences and international poetry festivals. She has a PhD in philosophy in Arabic literature.

Her books include the poetry collections *My Sorrow's Reward from His Collar* and *Zahr* (*Flowers*), as well as two books of criticism: *The Dialectic of Poetry and Prose in Modernist Poetry*, and *The Poetics of the Prose Poem*. Additionally, she's released a children's book, *Sultan and Shanidar*. Hanaa teaches at the University of Mosul.

ALI, SOUZAN is from Syria. She received a BA in psychology from Damascus University and a graduate degree from the Faculty of Information and Journalism, Damascus University. Her works include four poetry collections and two printed plays: *The Woman in My Mouth*, published by the Mediterranean Publishing House in 2019, and *I Want to Kill You in a Place That Loves Us*, published by Merritt Publishing House in 2021. Her book *When We Were Home*, which was part of the Women's Poetry Series presented and supervised by Adonis, was published by Dar al-Takween in 2024. As well, her texts have been published by the English-Arabic Library, a platform that translates and publishes books online. She is a poet, writer, and theater director.

ALMUBARK, HUDA is from Saudi Arabia. Her writings include two books: *dhabaabiya mut'ammida fii kamera almahmuul* (*An Intentional Fog on Mobile Phone's Camera*) in 2014, and *inzilaaq* (*Sliding*) in 2019. She currently works as a physical therapist at King Faisal Specialty Hospital in Riyadh.

ALSEBAIY, IMAN is from Egypt. Her publications include a collection of poetry, *Rosy Losses*, and a collection of stories, *I Am Alone Today*. Several of her literary and critical writings were published on Arab and Egyptian websites and journals.

BAGHDADI, SAMIRA is from Iraq. She received her MA in English language. Her writings include a collection of short stories, *laylat zafaafi* (*My Wedding Night*), published by Dar al-Warraq, and a novel translated into Arabic, *devdas* (*Devedas*).

BEN RHOUMA, SALWA is from Tunisia. Her writings include four poetry collections: *Wishes*, published by Al-Abr Publishing House in 2005; *Thikra Al-Ati*

(*Next Memory*), published by Al-Abr Publishing House in 2009; *We Decided to Extend the Life of Love*, published by Al Arabia Publishing and Printing House in 2018; and *Massacre Poems*, published by Dar Al-Masar Press of the Tunisian Writers Union in 2019. She is a member of the World Poets Movement in Chile and the Sfax Consulate. She has participated in several sessions of the Sfax International Festival. She had a poetry exhibit in several versions (Romance 1, 2, and 3), a poetry recitation employing music, and poetry clips broadcast on Tunisian TV channels.

BENNIS, FATIMA is from Morocco. Her writings include *law'at alhuruub* (*Agony of Escape*), in Tetouan (Morocco), 2004; *been thiraa'ay qamar* (*Between Arms of a Moon*), in Cairo, 2008; *taif nabi* (*A Vision of a Prophet*), in Beirut, 2011; *ala haafet omar haab* (*On Omar Haab's Edge*), in Tunisia, 2016; and *Alborde de una vida fugitiva*, published by the Mohammed VI Center for Dialogue of Civilizations, Chile, in 2017. She won a Creativity Award from the Alnoor Foundation, Sweden, in 2008.

CHAKAROUN, SUZANNE is from Lebanon. Her works include *A Manifesto of Death in a Fish Memory*, published by Nelson Printing House in 2016. Poems from this book were translated into German as part of an anthology of Lebanese women poets project with 37 other Lebanese poets in the book *The World in Our Eyes. Die welt in unseren Augen- Libanesische frauenanthologie*, published by Shaker Printing House, Aachen, Germany, which was co-translated by Cornelia Zierat and Sarjoun Karam. She currently works as an instructor at the College of Architecture and Fine Arts, Lebanese University, first branch, Al Hadat. She is a fine artist and a researcher.

DHAHRI, MEJDA is from Tunisia. Her works include *taraanim almaa'* (*Water Psalms*) in 2010 and *maa tayasara min suuratiha* (*What's Seen of Her Picture*) in 2015, and joint collections in Tunisia and abroad including *rabi' aliqhiwan* (*Chrysanthemum Spring*) in Egypt and *maraatij baab albahr* (*Vibrations of Sea Water*) in Tunisia. Many of her works have been translated into English, French, Italian, and Persian. She currently works as a pedagogical assistant in elementary-level education and is a civil society activist.

FADHIL, RASHA is from Iraq. She is an award-winning short-story writer, poet, novelist, playwright, and journalist. She is currently a PhD candidate at University of Brighton, UK, and her research focuses on the intersection of digital culture and gender identities in posthuman theatre. She was born in Basra in 1975 and spent her childhood there, attended college and lived for a time in Tikrit. She holds a BA in English from the University of Tikrit and was awarded a certificate in International Journalism and Media Studies from the Institute of Arab Strategy in Beirut in 2008. Five of her books, consisting of collections of short stories, poetry, and criticism, have been published in Cairo and Syria. She is a member of the Federation of Writers in Iraq, the advisory board of the Palace of Culture and Arts in Salah al-Din, and the International PEN Club in Berlin. She has worked for the Red Crescent and the Red Cross in Iraq at the Department of Prisoners and Detainees as well as in health education addressing AIDS prevention.

HADDAD, HANNAN is from Jordan. She received her high school diploma and did training courses in mathematics. Her writings include about 400 poems and more than 100 poetic thoughts. She previously worked as a math teacher in middle and elementary schools.

HANI AL-HAJJAR, SUZANNAH is originally from Syria and currently lives in the US. She holds a BA in medicine from Damascus University and an MA in public health from the University of New Hampshire in the US. She currently serves as the president of the American Druze Society (ADS) Boston chapter, is a member of the Women's Auxiliary Committee of the ADS, and holds the position of chair of culture preservation in the Swaida American Society.

HANNA, JACKLEEN (pen name Jackleen Salam) is originally from Syria and currently lives in Canada. She studied electrical engineering at Aleppo University. Her poetry collection *One Body and a Thousand Edge* was nominated for the most prestigious Arabic literature prize in the Middle East and diaspora, the Al Sheikh Zayed Prize, in 2016. Publications include *Conversations on the Mirrors of Migration*, an electronic collection of articles and 30 interviews with Canadian and Arab writers including John Ralston Saul, Rawi Hag, Walid Al Khashab, and others, published by *Winged Frog* in 2023; *One Body and a Thousand Edge,* published by Hamaleel, United Arab Emirates, in 2016; *The Inkwell Is a Female*, published by Alnahda Alarabia in 2009; *Suspicious Dancing*, published by Arabia lil Uloom in 2005, reprinted in 2022 as *She Nurtures the Clouds with Oranges*; *Crystal*, published by Al Kunooz Aladabia in 2001; and *The Fall is Shedding Mulberry Leaves*, electronically published by Almarava Althaafia in 2001. She is a member of the Writers in Exile Group and is a member of the Writer's Union of Canada and PEN Canada.

AL-HARBA, SALMA ABDUL HUSSEIN is from Iraq. She received her high diploma in English from the British Council in Baghdad in 1990. Her writings include *Raheel al-Nawaris* (*The Seagulls' Departure*), published by Dar Djlah in 2013, and *Sada Nayat* (*Echoes of Flutes*), also published by Dar Djlah in 2014. Her translated work has been published in *Talking Writing* magazine. Currently, she is a teacher of English in Basra.

HASSAN, FALEEHA is originally from Iraq and now lives in the US. She is a poet, teacher, editor, writer, and playwrite. She received her MA in Arabic literature, and has published 25 books. Her poems have been translated into English, Turkmen, Bosavi, Indian, French, Italian, German, Kurdish, Spanish, Korean, Greek, Serbian, Albanian, Pakistani, Malayalam, and Odia. She received many awards in Iraq and throughout the Middle East for her poetry and short stories. Her poems and short stories have been published in many American magazines. Awards include the Pushcart Prize in 2019, and she was a Pulitzer Prize nominee in 2018.

HUSSAIN, ASMAA is from Egypt. She holds a BA in journalism and an MA in journalism production. She is a narrator, poet, and translator. Her works include a collection of stories, *uthriyya* (*Virginity*), published by Dar Mira, in 2012; *fushat bowayka* (*Bowayka Space*), published by Dar Fasla Publishing, in 2018; and a collection of poems, *ajmal alwuhuush allati 'aththat ruuhi* (*The Most Gorgeous Beasts that Bit My Soul*), published by Dar Rawaashin in 2019.

Her first collection, *nisaa yas'ab hubbahum* (*Women Hard to Love*), has been recently translated into English. Her story *lawn algharaq fii famii* ("Drowning Color in My Mouth") was shortlisted for the Elizabeth Jolley Story Prize and Maslakiya Women Literature Prize.

HUSSEIN, AZHAR ALI is from Iraq. She is a poet, short story writer, journalist, actress, film director, and scenarist. She works as a program producer for Alhurra TV. She is the author of numerous works of poetry, fiction, and film including *Taheta Sama Ukhra* (*Under Another Sky*) and *Mirath al-Dima* (*Legacy of Blood*). Her translated work has appeared in *Consequence Forum*.

JANEM, ATAF is from Jordan. She graduated from Al Yarmouk University, Department of Arabic Language, and worked as a teacher in Jordan, Yemen, and the United Arab Emirates. She is a member of the Jordanian Writers Association and the Arab Writers Union. Her publications include the poetry collections *For a Time to Come* (Jordanian Writers Association, 1988), *Threshold for Dreaming, Oh Kernels!* (Ministry of Culture, 1993), *Remorse of a Tree* (Amman Municipality's Cultural Department, 2003), *Butterfly Orbit* (Ministry of Culture, 2017), and the story collection *The Salvation Sign* (Dar Fadaa'at, 2017).

AL-KATIB, NADIA is from Iraq. She was born in Dohuk in 1968 and has a PhD in biology from the University of Tikrit. She is currently a teacher, poet, and short-story writer. Among her works is a collection of poetry, *Al-Tawqi': Ghaima* (*Signature: Cloud*). Her translated work has appeared in *The Common*

KHOURY, NESRIN EKRAM is from Syria. She holds a degree in civil engineering. Her publications include *bi-jarrat harb waahida* (*With the Stroke of One War*), published by Dar altakwiin, in 2015; *waadi qandiil* (*Qandil Valley*), published by Almutawassit in 2017; and *arkul albayt wa akhruj* (*I Kick Off the House and Go*), published by Dar Ninevah in 2019. She contributed to several publications including a Syrian Poets anthology, *The Love and War*, translated into French by Dar; *Le Temps Des Cerises*, the 5th edition of the American periodical *Life and Legends,* published in 2017; *Amaravati Poetic Prism,* published in India in 2017; *World Healing, World Peace Anthology,* published by Inner Child Press, USA, in 2018; *anna allathi anntum (I Am Whom You Are)*; and a bilingual Arabic-Catalonian publication of six Syrian poets, published in Barcelona in 2019. She is a former writer-in-residence at Casa Mediterraneo, Alicante, Spain (2018) and contributed to the Arabic Language Festival at Catholic University of Milano (2019).

MAHMOD, DIMA is from Egypt. She received a BS in computers and statistics. Her publications include *thafaa'ir ruuh (Braids of a Soul),* published by Dar aladham, 2015, and *Iushaakis alufuq bi-kamanja (I Quarrel with Horizon with a Violin),* published by Dar alayn, 2017. Many of her texts have been translated into English, French, Spanish, and Portuguese and published in several websites, magazines, and anthologies in these languages.

MAHMOUD, HODA ABDELKADER is from Egypt.

MANSOUR, FATIMA is from Lebanon. Her publications include *min wahy alquyuud (Inspiration of Restrictions), imra'a min fasiilat ash-shams (A Woman of a Sunny Type), heenama yuhalliq alfiniq biqiitha sumariyya (When the Phoenix Flies with a Sumerian Harp), untha ala ghayma (A Female on a Cloud), irti'aashaat aashiqa (Tremors of a Lover), ibhaar fii sutuur mu'taabi' (Sailing on Paved Lines), huruuf wa hawaajis (Letters and Concerns),* a joint collection with Moroccan writer Fatima bu Haraka titled *One Hundred Poets from the Arab World,* and in *The Great Encyclopedia of Arab Poets* by Fatima bu Haraka, a selected Arab feminist literature anthology.

EL-MARMOUKE, ZAKIA is from Morocco. She teaches French literature, has published five poetry collections, and is the director of Rabitat Al-Ebdaa' min Ajl Assalam (Association of Creativity for Peace). She resides in Morocco.

MASRWEH, EMAN is from Palestine. Her publications include *ana hadath wa majzara (I Am an Event and a Massacre)* in 1996; *hajar silaahi (A Stone is My Weapon*), published by the Palestinian Writers Union in 2002; *sariir alqamar* (*The Moon's Bed*) in 2010; *batuul lughati* (*Maiden is My Language*) in 2011; *dumuu' alhabaq* (*Basil's Tears*) in 2012; *araa'is alfajr* (*Dawn Brides*), published by the Palestinian Ministry of Culture [2012 or 2013]; *huna watan* (*Here Is Home*), published by Fadhaa'at Amman in 2013; *min khawaatiri* (*Some of My Thoughts*), in 2013; *bukaa'iyyat alwadaa' alakhiir* (*Lamentations of Final Farewell*) in 2013; *almalhama almuhammadiyya* (*Muhammadan Epic*), published by Alsirat Press in 2014; *aukobediya* (*Aucopedia*) in 2014; *Sulaaf* (*Sulaf*), published by Bayt Alshi'r in 2015; *thumaaniyyat maqdisiyya* (*Eighths Jerusalemite*), published by the Ansar aldhaad Foundation, in 2016; *I'tiqaal alharf laa ya'ni alqasiida* (*Arresting the Letter Doesn't Mean the Poem*) in 2016; *li-lhulm baqiyya* (*To be Continued*), published by Ash-sham press, in 2016; *zahra wamdaat shi'riyya* (*Flower of Poetical Sparkles*), published by the Ansar aldhaad Foundation in 2017; *fii intidhaar aldhaw'* (*Waiting for Light*) in 2017and *tarhat li-arus al-jaliil* (*A Veil for a Galilee Bride*), in 2018.

MOSTAFA, RAGHDA is from Egypt. She graduated from the College of Civil Engineering, Asyut University, in 2010. Her publications include *sarrubi lihawaasik* (*Let Me through to Your Senses*), published by the Ibdaat series of the General Organization of Culture Palaces in 2018. Her poetic collection was the runner-up for the Akhbar Aladab Prize, in the formal Arabic category, in 2017. Her poems are frequently published by literary magazines and newspapers.

AL MUFTI, NERMEEN is from Iraq. She was born in Kirkuk in 1959 and has a BA in translation from Mustansiriya University, Baghdad. Her diploma in journalism is from the International School of Journalists IOJ in Budapest, Hungary; and her MA in political science is from Mustansiriya University. She is a human rights activist, journalist, poet, and short-story writer. Among her works are *The Diaries of the Dying Man: Short Stories*, and *Wounds in the Palm Tree: Stories of the Eyewitness in Iraq*. Her translated work has appeared in *The Common*.

ALNAHI, KHAWLA JASIM is from Iraq. She is a journalist, translator, and news editor. Her writings include two story collections: *laa'iha bi-asmaa' almalaa'ika* (*A List of Angels' Names*), in 2013, and *jinuub khat 33* (*Line 33 South*), in 2019. Her story *sahib almizan* (*The Scale Owner*) was published in *laa'ibu as-sard* (*Players of Narration*) in Basra in 2015. She is a member of the Iraq Writers Union.

SALAMEH, AMIRA is from Syria. She has published and won awards for her poetry, children's stories, and puppet theater; as well, she writes theatrical scripts and directs plays for the Cultural Center in Latakia.

AL SAYED, LAYLA is from Bahrain. Her writings include: *marrana hunaak* (*We Passed There*), published by the Arts and Culture Authority in Bahrain in collaboration with Dar Alarabiya; *Amman* (*Who Inherits the Smile of Mine*), a translation of *We Passed There* in addition to other new poems translated into English, Spanish, and German; *mathaq aluzla* (*Taste of Isolation*), published by Dar Fradays in 2006; *malyaan kaffi hibr* (*The Palm of My Hand) is Full of Ink*), published by Dar Nifro in 2007; *da' tayrak yabtahij* (*Let Your Bird Rejoice*), published by Dar Mas'a in 2011; *karaz wa matar* (*Cherry and Rain*), published by Dar Aljamal in 2013; a joint digital collection with Iman Masiri titled *israaf fii aj-jiluus ma'a allay* (*Excessive Sitting Down with Night*) published in 2022; *nisf mukhadati wa nahaari kullahu* (*Half of My Pillow and All My Days*), published by Dar Abjad in 2023; and a joint collection with poets Ahmed Alajmi and Iman Masiri, *samt bi-uyuun mulawwana* (*Silence of Colored Eyes*), published by Dar Bahr Damascus in 2023. She has participated in many world festivals such as the Maiden Festival in Colombia in 2005, and contributed a story, *alharisa* (Harissa), to the Milan Expo in 2015, and to the World Poetry Encyclopedia *shi'r shajarat alaalam* (*World Poetry Tree*) launched by the United Arab Emirates-hosted Expo 2020. She contributed to the 21st Century's Greatest Human Poetry Epic, in collaboration with 85 poets from around the world. She won a prize in the Tulliola-Renato Filippelli Contest in 2019.

AL SHAYBANI, SUMIA is from Kuwait. Her writings include *harisat an-nakhil* (*The Palm Tree Guard*), *nisf li-lqathifa* (*Half for a Bomb*), and *hiyya allati ra'at* (*She Is the One Who Saw*).

SHOSHA, ZIZI is from Egypt. Her writings include *ghurabaa' alaqu bi-hithaaii* (*Strangers Got Stuck in My Shoes*), published by the General Organization of Culture Palaces in 2017, and *ismah li-llayl bi-d-dukhuul* (*I Allow Night to Enter*), published by Almutawassit in 2019. Her poetry book *malaabis jadiida li-lmawta* (*New Clothes for the Dead*) won the Literature News Award in 2017. Her third poetry collection, *maqha laa ya'rifahu ahad* (*A Coffeehouse that No One Knows*), was published by the General Egyptian Book Association in 2020. Her poems have been published in international and Arab journals and newspapers and she has participated in several literary events and conferences. Her translated work has appeared in *Talking Writing* magazine.

SOLIMAN, MARIAM is from Egypt. She received her BA from the Communication Department of Ain Shams University. Her works include *rapsody* (*Rhapsody*), published by Dar Afaq in 2011.

AL-ZABEDY, ELHAM NASSER is from Iraq. She is a poet, visual artist, and women's rights advocate. Born in Baghdad, she graduated from the Institute of Fine Arts, Music Department, in Basra. She is a leading figure in cultural activism, founding and running the Lotus Cultural Women's League. She serves as a member of the international project Her Story Is with artist Amy Miller. Her literary contributions encompass the poetry collections *Whispers of the Walnut Tree* (2008) and *Shores of the Sparrows* (2012).

www.ingramcontent.com/pod-product-compliance
Lightning Source LLC
Chambersburg PA
CBHW070416210825
31317CB00020B/241